GOD
IN THE MIDST OF
CHANGE

Wisdom for Confusing Times

Diarmuid O'Murchu, MSC

ORBIS BOOKS
Maryknoll, New York 10545

Founded in 1970, Orbis Books endeavors to publish works that enlighten the mind, nourish the spirit, and challenge the conscience. The publishing arm of the Maryknoll Fathers and Brothers, Orbis seeks to explore the global dimensions of the Christian faith and mission, to invite dialogue with diverse cultures and religious traditions, and to serve the cause of reconciliation and peace. The books published reflect the views of their authors and do not represent the official position of the Maryknoll Society. To learn more about Maryknoll and Orbis Books, please visit our website at www.maryknollsociety.org.

Copyright © 2012 by Claretian Publications

Originally published in the Philippines by **Claretian Publications**, a division of **Claretian Communications Foundation, Inc**.
U.P. P.O. Box 4, Diliman 1101 Quezon City, Philippines
Tel.: (02) 921-3984 • Fax: (02) 921-6205
cci@claret.org • ccfi@claretphilippines.com
www.claretianpublications.com

First published in North America by Orbis Books, Maryknoll, New York 10545-0302.
Manufactured in the United States of America.

Layout: Novel Bernabe P. Estillore.

Library of Congress Cataloging-in-Publication Data

O'Murchu, Diarmuid.
God in the midst of change : wisdom for confusing times / Diarmuid O'Murchu.
 pages cm
 Includes bibliographical references.
 ISBN 978-1-62698-041-9 (pbk.)
 1. Evolution--Religious aspects--Christianity. 2. Change--Religious aspects--Christianity. 3. Christianity and culture. I. Title.
BT712.O23 2013
261--dc22

2013005213

Contents

Introduction

Millions of people have their heads buried in the quick sands of our changing world. Changing it is - and it will continue to do so. We are undergoing one of those evolutionary shifts that cannot and will not be arrested. Most people don't know what is really going on, and most do not want to know.

This book is aimed at those who do want to know, those sufficiently sensitized to the dislocation all around us, yet capable of discerning that the disintegration will give way to transformation, although the implications are far from clear.

It is a time for an enormous sense of trust, not so much in humanity itself –which for the greater part still lives in the dark, nor in the God who rules from on high, who has lost credibility on a massive scale in recent decades - but rather in *the evolving wisdom of creation itself*. During its four billion year history our earth has been through several evolutionary transformations, and survived in every case. It is this universal will-to-life that commands credibility for the seekers-after-truth in our time.

Major evolutionary shifts are characterized by two features: firstly, a painful chaotic dying to what we have known, loved and cherished; secondly, an eager but unclear sense of anticipation that there is something radically new breaking through on a not so distant future horizon. And in such times, we all stand in between (a third feature if you wish): a liminal space, marked by an unfamiliar mix of chaos and creativity. Negotiating our way through this dislocating experience requires a multi-disciplinary wisdom, with a creative spirituality as its central inspiration. What that multi-disciplinary spirituality looks like is the primary focus of this book.

The book consists of three parts, marking the three features as identified above. The first part is an analysis of the inherited wisdom with its increasingly dysfunctional articulations in terms of behavior, system and structure (institution). I describe these as *distortions*. These are major aspects of our everyday world, which at one time are useful and effective, but increasingly are now unable to deliver meaning or a sense of purpose. Part One is therefore an attempt at naming major aspects of the painful letting-go.

In the second part of the book, I outline some examples of the breakdown that is happening all around us, leaving many people disoriented and confused. We don't know what or who to trust anymore. I try to name some of the features that leave so many people feeling dislocated and disillusioned. By naming and clarifying what is actually going on, we can deal with it in a more engaging way rather than merely ignoring it, or seeking to escape it by turning to many of the popular compensations of our time: shopping, gambling, hedonism, recreational drugs.

The third part of the book is the most ambitious. To some this may seem esoteric and overly idealistic as I am proposing that evolution itself is our best guide at this dislocating, transformative time. The universe (and God) knows what it's about. It is a gamble we must take, both for our present sanity and future hope. I open up some suggestive pathways into a new paradigm – many of which have been named in recent times by several other cultural visionaries. And I briefly outline the personal and systemic implications for all of us who choose to embrace the new transformation.

At this time, we are living through a classic paradigm shift! Many suggest it is pointless to try and make sense of it. Yet, I suggest there are more than enough hints and signals for us to begin a process of discernment: "What might the creative Spirit be up to?" And that is all I am attempting in this book: *to offer initial insights and namings of what is transpiring,* enough to create a cultural infrastructure on the basis of which those ready to move forward can begin the painful but life-giving task of being co-evolutionary catalysts for the new future awakening in our midst.I am offering brief insights into movements of our time that engage each and every one of us. I trust the material will be useful as a resource for deeper personal reflection, and for empowering dialogue with other soul-searchers, sharing the journey with us. I suspect it is those of us who remain faithful to the search — who keep our minds and hearts open in reading the signs of our time — are the ones who will contribute most to the eventual breakthrough. Welcome to the exploration!

This is a Reader-Friendly Book:

- There no Chapters—only Sections

- Each Section is quite short—and can be read in less than 30 minutes

- Each Section is focused on one central idea, briefly outlined, with suggestions for further exploration.

- The style is one of teasing the reader into further discovery, wetting your appetite to learn more.

- The further learning is your responsibility, to be embraced in accordance with your wisdom and intelligence, and not dictated by me, the author.

- This approach is encouraged today by several advocates of Adult Learning.

- You are encouraged to browse online resource material, as well as other learning facilities, that may help to deepen your wisdom and knowledge.

- In participative learning, we distinguish between the academic and the intellectual, reminding ourselves that everybody is endowed with wisdom and intellect

- Enjoy the read—and kindly pass on the book—or its wisdom, to friends and colleagues.

Part One:

NAMING INHERITED DISTORTIONS

The planet is being exhausted in the excessive exploitation of natural resources. Not only is the functioning of the human community out of alignment with the functioning of the planet, but also the human community has become a predator draining the life of its host.

Thomas Berry

At the heart of the global pathology dominating the Earth is a conception of power as domination.

Mark Hathaway & Leonardo Boff.

First Benchmark: *Confronting distortions*

F ew can deny the upheaval and chaos in the world today. It is increasingly obvious that many things are falling apart. And those entrusted with governance, in whom millions invest so much trust –along with power and money –are often confused in their perceptions and decisions. Meanwhile, anarchic forces –politically, economically, socially, and even religiously –begin to fill the chaotic vacuum. And often they create more havoc than what already prevails.

The disorientation and disillusionment is made all the worse by the denial in which we are immersed. This denial pertains particularly to *a set of assumptions*, still considered sacred, and fiercely protected by those in power. But those of us at the receiving end of power also invest deeply in these assumptions. Hence, this is the reason why we continue to trust those formally in authority, even when it becomes unambiguously clear that they are fumbling around in the dark, and are probably no better than ourselves in their understanding of what is going on.

Central to the distorted assumptions that I outline in Part One of this book is a religious ideology far more deeply rooted than most of us suspect. In the Western world, we often encounter atheistic intellectuals who forthrightly denounce and reject religion, but go on to create another ideology (often a scientific one), at least as powerful and as intransigent as the one they have rejected. For Western readers, the biologist, Richard Dawkins (of selfish gene repute), springs to mind. These days, the high priests of religion are often replaced by the high priests of science, economics, or globalization.

Religiously, politically, economically and socially –it is the same ideologue who commands the high ground, and for several centuries has lured humans into passivity and co-dependence. And the resulting corrupt anthropocentrism –man as the measure of all things – has also taken a heavy toll on the living Earth itself. In due course, evolution will remove these distortions; if humans can participate in that process, we become much more readily - and consciously - empowered to embrace evolution's forward movement. And then hope can become much more visible – a virtue so urgently needed in the despondent times in which we live.

1. *The Two-thousand-Year Hallmark*

The unquestioned assumption: *To manage and control, we need specific time limits. According to the prevailing wisdom, everything of importance has happened in the past two thousand years.*

There is so much we want to do, and so much expected of us, we never seem to have enough time at our disposal. Something tells us we should be able to manage time more efficiently, yet we never seem to get there. Time always beats us to the target. We expend much energy battling with time, but it seems like a battle in vain. So, we just get on with it, and make the best of what is at our disposal.

Time denotes a kind of fatalism, one we tolerate rather than review reflectively. And we are quite mechanistic in our approach to time. We quantify every undertaking and judge success by how much money or power we accumulate within a specific time scale. Like many other aspects of our bewildering world today, we have consigned time to a reductionistic, rational process. We have stripped time of its mystery and awesome grandeur.

The two-thousand-year benchmark

Time plays a significant role in the way we understand our world, but our experience of time is largely subconscious. Currently most humans attribute enormous significance to the two-thousand-year benchmark, but are largely unaware of how it impacts on their lives.

Although this benchmark is generated by the Christian religion it has totally outlived its religious context and has assumed a strong cultural significance. Even the Chinese who celebrate a different timing for each New Year, adopt the two-thousand-year benchmark when it comes to trade and global financial transactions.

As a cultural point of reference, millions around our world assume that nothing of significance happened before the date of 2,000 years ago, while after it, it is widely assumed, that true civilization only began to develop and flourish. This conviction is initially derived from the conventional understanding of the Christian faith. God's real engagement with the human race takes place in and through Jesus, who lived, died and was "raised from the dead" about 2,000 years ago. According to conventional Christian theology, that date marks the beginning of "salvation" not just for Christians, but also for all humanity. And the most reliable knowledge of God's will for humanity (called *revelation*) also arises from the exemplary events of that time-line.

The reader will readily recognize the strong anthropocentric undercurrent. The two-thousand-year benchmark sees humanity as the pinnacle of creation. Everything before that time was leading up to the human. Only the human really matters. The great eons of evolutionary unfolding, through the cosmic and planetary trajectories, are of secondary importance, and not really significant for how we measure historical time or how we engage with it.

Scientific ambivalence

In the realm of practical science, we also adopt the two-thousand-year benchmark — largely unaware of its gaping inconsistencies. Despite the now widespread knowledge of a cosmos of 13.7 billion years and an Earth-planet of 3.8 billion, rarely do we embrace those time-horizons in our engagement with daily life. And when science does accommodate some of our ancient cosmic and planetary wisdom, it tends to be used as a means of bolstering our functional worldview that has evolved from more recent datings.

These are some of the significant dates that impact on our contemporary worldview:

> *13.7 billion years*: Origin of the universe we know today.
>
> *4.00 billion years*: Evolution of our home planet, the Earth.
>
> *2.00 billion years ago*: Emergence of the first bacteria, the foundations of organic life.
>
> *7 million years ago*: Emergence of the first humans.

While science castigates, and sometimes mocks, religion, for its narrow reductionistic views, science itself seems to be caught in the horns of an embarrassing dilemma. Science stretches our time-horizons, opening us up to the wonders of the larger creation, in ways that often leaves religion limping in cultural irrelevance. Yet, the inherited religious timeframe of the 2,000 years seems to command a far stronger allegiance than science, a contradiction often played out in the creationist-evolutionist debacle in the United States of America and elsewhere.

Educational processes also seem to be caught in this conceptual dilemma. Many sciences such as mathematics, physics, and chemistry are based on influential ideas developed over the past 2,000 years. And for much of that time, religion (and theology) dictated the intellectual context and the capacity for understanding. Not until the twentieth century did the more ancient dates for the other great religions – Hinduism, Buddhism, etc. —carry any significance for Western educators. Even to this day, other religions are often taught as being secondary and inferior to the Christian story.

Controlling time

Time is a dimension of human experience that many people never even think about. Clock-time, the twenty-four hour cycle, dominates and controls our lives. Paradoxically we spend a great deal of energy managing time as we strive to be in control of our lives and our world.

Our sense of time is distinctly functional, particularly in how we handle the social, political and economic dimensions of life. It is a measurement within which things can be accomplished. Beginnings and endings are significant, while quantity determines how useful time is for us. Few people realize that this modern approach to time is quite a recent development, very different to how we understood time, and engaged with it, throughout our evolutionary story of seven million years. (More in O'Murchu 2009).

Flowing with the rhythm of time has been our experience for most of human history. Time had a cyclic sense interpreted through the movement of sun, moon and stars. Time was broken down into day, night and the seasons; the latter was discerned mainly through the fertility of the earth and the behavior of birds and animals. Past, present and future were viewed more as a continuum. Destiny was in the hands of an embracing life force known to many indigenous peoples as The Great Spirit. (More in O'Murchu 2012).

Rhythm, flow and cycle determined destiny and its meaning. People were not too worried what it all meant. Although we think that faith in a personal deity did not exist nonetheless the enveloping sense of mystery within which everything was held was deemed to be fundamentally benign. Traces of this sense of time can still be detected among contemporary indigenous peoples, while also being more conducive to the pace of life known to millions living in Africa and Asia.

The future of time

Obviously, we are not going to revert to the idyllic scenario outlined above. Evolution never regresses. Despite its practical usefulness, however, our current approach to time, with so much panic, accelerated pace and fierce competition, is not congenial to the flowering of human potential. And the addictive allegiance to the two-thousand-year benchmark is deadening and suffocating for the human spirit.

The re-awakening of spirituality in the 20th century – more specifically, a new wave of mystical fervor – arises from a human yearning to live differently upon planet Earth, savor its natural endowments and cherish its enriching beauty. In a word, we need to slow down! Doctors have been telling us that, so have psychotherapists, and the many other specialists we consult about our stress and weariness. Instinctively, many people are also trying to change the pace and intensity of daily life, and the popularity of Eastern meditation practices in recent decades has made an important contribution, bringing sanity and sanctity into our serrated, fragmented existence.

A sense of time is integral to all worldviews. The prevailing view, characterized by the two-thousand-year benchmark, is too narrow and reductionistic to be useful for the future. It also carries excessive religious and patriarchal baggage (examined in later Sections). At this time of major transition, we can ill afford to burden ourselves like that. We need to outgrow the time-limitations we have inherited so that our spirits – along with our minds and bodies – can soar towards more expansive horizons where we can embrace the empowering potential of deep time.

Inspired by this expansive view, we stand a much better chance to embrace the profound and turbulent changes which evolution is inaugurating in our rapidly changing world. We are likely to better understand what is unfolding all around us, and engage the evolving process with greater wisdom, integrity and hope.

2. *When Civilization Becomes Suspicious*

The unquestioned assumption: *That which we can manage and control belongs to recent millennia, when humans left behind a kind of primitive ignorance, and became rationally aware, i.e., civilized.*

Civilization is a word to be used with caution. We all assume we know what the word means, but in truth its meaning is a kind of cultural myopia that remains largely unexamined. In daily usage, it denotes ways of behaving characterized by civility, responsibility, due care, and respect for the other. Frequently, however, it carries an air of arrogance and superiority, to distinguish those who are civilized from those who belong to cultures or situations deemed to be primitive, barbaric and inferior to those of us who belong to more developed and advanced cultures.

In times of massive change, the creative chaos is often demonized because of a perceived threat to our civilized world. Thus, the need to discern the deeper meaning of what is transpiring is undermined by negative reaction. Sometimes, we invoke labels –such as Postmodernism, or New Age –to demonize those who instigate change. The desire to cling on to the established order is in fact the very thing that hinders a more comprehensive and civilized way of dealing with the transition taking place.

Civilization, as officially defined, has a particularly distorted history. All the major sciences use terms such as: the dawn, the rise, the beginnings, of civilization. In every case, civilization is traced to a particular historical moment, around 7,000 years ago, and to two dominant events unfolding around that time:

-The development of *writing* in the Sumerian culture, located primarily in the Tigris-Euphrates valley; and

-The evolution of *the first cities* around the same time, located more to the West of the Tigris-Euphrates valley, contemporary Syria, Israel and Palestine.

Civilization and human management

Why do scholars of all (certainly most) disciplines agree on this definition of civilization? Nobody seems to have answered that question; indeed, few seem to have asked it! One wonders if it is not another manifestation of the patriarchal desire to mange and control. Writing things down, and the ability to check written records, keeps information within boundaries that are more easily managed and controlled. And cities keep people more centrally located, socially organized, and politically more streamlined.

Undoubtedly, the evolution of writing and urbanization marks a new evolutionary threshold, highlighting more advanced and sophisticated abilities in the human species. And this seems to be the crux in which world viewing becomes misguided. Before this time, it is assumed that humans were essentially uncivilized, primitive, violent, barbaric, and somehow incomplete. We disparage, and therefore tend to dismiss, all the richness and depth in our evolutionary unfolding of the previous *7 million* years. We short-circuit and jeopardize the true story to which we belong as human beings.

Scholars also date the origin of settled habitats to this time. The hunter-gatherers wandered less, and turned their attention to the cultivation of root crops and the domestication of cattle. Social organization moved more towards settled tribes and clans, with the beginnings of social stratification, characterized particularly by male patriarchal dominance. Conditions more conducive to our modern understanding of life became normative, thus suggesting to contemporary scholars that humans were becoming more advanced and sophisticated.

The scholars often fail to note that the previous more organic connection with the earth and the wider creation was compromised and significantly curtailed. Humans came to be seen as a superior breed and progressively set themselves up – and over – the rest of creation. The gradual objectification of nature – treating everything as a useful commodity – began to evolve. It was deemed to be necessary for the civilized progress. But what counted as progress for humanity, proved to have disastrous consequences for the earth-human relationship.

To this day, we adopt the demarcation line between history and pre-history, the latter referring to what transpired and developed before the rise of "civilization" and widely regarded as being inferior to what emerged thereafter. We have inherited another dysfunctional worldview, or at least a major dimension of our way of seeing the world, which few people feel a need to question or re-examine.

A Western bias

Ever since the sixteenth century, Europe was deemed to be the cultural heartland of the entire planet. From Europe emanated the industrial revolution, the epitome of civilized progress. All the major colonizing forces in the nineteenth and twentieth centuries were Europeans, particularly the British, Spanish and Dutch. From Europe the Christian missionaries went forth to convert the uncivilized pagans throughout the rest of the planet. And in the later half of the twentieth century, developmental strategies to aid the poor and impoverished of the Southern hemisphere emulated those tried and tested in the West; in a number of cases indigenous resources were disenfranchised, leaving local peoples confused and disempowered.

The Western worldview, seeking to develop all the other inferior peoples and cultures, was charged with an arrogance and consequent violence that has left in its wake a great deal of exploitation, slavery, oppression, racism and sectarianism. Europeans acted like divine saviors and tended to treat other peoples and cultures with disdain. And the imperialism continues in the modern guise of *globalization,* which paradoxically is no longer Western-driven, as new commerce-centers, like Brazil and China, come to the fore.

Now the tide is beginning to turn. Colonialism is largely a spent force, politically speaking. However, it is still quite virulent as an economic force in the movement known as globalization. During the twentieth century, the pendulum of world power swung from Europe to the United States, and in the early twenty-first century is rapidly shifting from the United States to China, India and Brazil. Meanwhile the repressed anger, resulting from Western oppression finds voice in fundamentalist Islam, mediated through organizations such as Al Qaida, with the United States as the primary target of attack. The worldview orchestrated through Western civilization has lost much of its credibility on the world stage.

Civilization is at a crossroads. In several cases, the old reliable guideposts are no longer capable of sustaining our evolution in either personal or planetary terms. Many of our major institutions are fraying at the edges and likely to implode due to their cultural intransigence. People have lost trust in those entrusted with leadership and responsible governance – in political, economic, social and religious fields. We don't expect creative resolutions from those in charge, nor indeed is there much evidence that those institutions can deliver to any significant degree the elements of a new civic order. Ours is a time of cultural depletion, a threadbare moment, a dark night of the collective soul. We would hope the dawn is not far behind, but truthfully, we have no idea. The best of all possible worlds is to trust the chaos!

It is no longer clear what we mean by *civilization*. What is clear is that the old identification with writing and urbanization has long outlived its usefulness. Yet, a disturbing fixation still prevails. All the cultural achievements of pre-civilized times, that is prior to some 5,000 years ago, tend to be labelled as uncivilized, primitive and barbaric. It is assumed that we had evolved into the mature civilized peoples we are today. Therefore, too much attention to these ancient times is perceived as a form of romantic nostalgia, not befitting our advanced wisdom.

Civilized religion

This arbitrary demarcation line –between civilized and uncivilized –marks a cultural distortion that seriously hinders our acquisition of a more integrated self-image. It leaves us with a restricted, stultified sense our humanity, devoid of the groundedness and creativity that sustained us over several thousands of years. And it also undermines the animist, nature-based spirituality through which we grew and flourished long before civilized religions evolved in our world.

The monotheistic religions –Judaism, Christianity and Islam - are generally considered to be more developed and civilized than those emerging from the Far East. Here lies a formidable challenge for all peoples living in Asia, and for Christians particularly. Monotheism emphasizes the superiority of the One God, who in all cases is unambiguously male. The patriarchal connotations are all too obvious. The major religions indigenous to the Orient – Hinduism, Buddhism, Sikhism – are more polytheistic in their belief, with Buddhism widely regarded as being non-theistic. This more formless belief system is deemed to be inferior (uncivilized or pre-civilized) to the great Western faiths.

Civilization –as defined above –is the critical issue here. Because it cherishes a value-system, more explicitly focused on the rational, linear and patriarchal, it fails to appreciate the symbolic diffused richness in the other great religions. All too quickly, the other faiths are denounced and dismissed as primitive and pagan. Correspondingly, the strong Eastern emphasis on meditation and interiority is also held to be suspect. Paradoxically, it many cases, a practice such as meditation gains a far wider credibility in the secular than in the religious sphere.

That which we cling on to –religiously and politically –needs a more critical evaluation. It is a distortion against evolution itself to deify any one set of values as civilized and categorize all others as inferior or primitive. This is not cultural relativism, but an attempt to live congruently with our evolving world, where civilized values and mores change in tune with evolutionary unfolding. Fluidity and flexibility, rather than dogmatic fixation, keep us closer to the truth that yields a deeper and more empowering meaning.

3. *The Patriarchal Will-to-Power*

The unquestioned assumption: *The hierarchal way of doing things is obvious from the natural world and clearly has been validated by how God rules the world. There is only one right way: from the top downward.*

Despite the extensive cultural liberalization evidenced throughout the world in the closing decades of the twentieth century, the central role of patriarchal authority still dominates the human landscape. Most forms of political government, the prevailing economic systems, religious institutions, and the basic structure of cultural socialization (namely, the family) are still unquestionably patriarchal. The line of command is from the top down, and the person at the top tends to be the dominant male.

We see an increasing number of women occupying this domineering space. Gendering the roles does not change its fundamental dynamism. Paradoxically, women too are easily lured into the cultural distortions that belong to power, domination and control. The patriarchal will-to-power has infiltrated human consciousness over several millennia and this can have adverse effects on men and women alike. In the past, women have been the primary victims of patriarchal disempowerment. Today, it seems to be the *living Earth* itself that is being victimized with men and women often colluding in such destructive domination.

Patriarchy: a brief history

Theorists of various disciplines tend to define *patriarchy* differently. Although broadly agreed on its essential features, they trace its history along varying lines, usually within the space of the past 5,000 years and frequently within the past 2,000 years. I suggest we need a much larger context to understand this phenomenon in its full virulence. I trace this most recent wave of patriarchal dominance to the shadow side of the Agricultural Revolution, an evolutionary emergence which itself is being reconsidered at the present time. (Previous waves may have existed about which we know nothing.)

Conventionally, we trace the rise of agriculture to about 10,000 years ago (c.8,000 BCE). Humans had been cultivating land and producing food for thousands, possibly millions, of years before then. However, for a range of reasons that have not been clearly delineated, across northern and central Europe (as we now know it), an accelerated wave of land domestication transpired about 10,000 years ago. Rapid growth in human population and the onset of a new ice age may have been the primary contributing factors to this novel development.

However, the religious validation of this patriarchal upsurge probably belongs to Northern Africa and the Middle East, rather than to the domestication of land in Europe. About 8,000 years ago (c.6,000 BCE), the freezing conditions reached Northern Africa, transforming a rich fertile plain into what we know today as the Sahara desert; it stretched eastward into what is now known as the Arabian desert. Prior to that time both North Africa and the Arabian Peninsula were a thriving fertile crescent. The onset of the ice age rapidly changed the entire landscape, resulting in upheaval and dislocation for human and animal alike. (More in Taylor 2005).

Humans seem to have responded as they had done in Europe. A new aggressive, male warrior caste came to the fore. A panic towards greater control became the guiding value. A new aggressiveness emerged, what Steve Taylor (2005) describes as an ego explosion. And it became progressively more militant and domineering.

To justify and validate the new dispensation, humans engineered a new God concept: *a ruling sky God*, who mandated humans to rule and govern as well. But for reasons that are difficult to discern, it was only some humans: namely males, who were deemed capable of such divinely mandated governance. The suppression of females, and their previous contribution to the development of the earth and its resources, seems to have been rapidly and brutally reinforced. We pick up the story in the next Section.

The patriarchal will-to-power

Although several social theorists criticize the patriarchal system, most also acknowledge its several achievements of civility, structure, organization and governance. It is hard to imagine any other system that could have achieved so much. But herein lies the dilemma. The patriarchal system is so designed and structured, it rarely allows for any alternatives to be considered, and when such allowance is made, the outcomes are closely vetted to ensure they do not undermine that which dominates and prevails. As we know today, patriarchal power is exemplary in its propensity for total control, infiltrating the cultural outlets of information, education, social policy and cultural values.

This pervasive, invasive controlling grip on power is often illustrated through the Duluth Wheel (http://www.theduluthmodel. org), indicating the subtle dynamics, often invisible to the general public, and indeed only selectively available even to the critical researcher. Although based solely on the domestic violence industry, the Duluth Wheel highlights dynamics extensively employed nationally and internationally to reinforce domination, power, and the values that ensure its self-perpetuation:

1. Lies, distortion and misinformation: Suppress the truth and distort the facts to the advantage of the power-holders, while simultaneously including some positive gestures to distract people from seeing the suppression.

2. Suppression of research: Only that which reinforces the governing ideology will be approved, often noticeable in sensitive issues such as the use of nuclear power.

3. Demonization and intolerance: ridicule, shame and if possible eliminate those who disagree.

4. Economic abuse: use money and funding as a power-tool, and a means to gain support, especially in political voting.

5. Exclusion: selective favoritism of those who are willing to collude, and exclusion of those who resist being co-opted.

6. Hijacking of feminism: Any form of alternative thinking or counter-cultural re-visioning will be viewed with suspicion, and frequently with ridicule.

Cultural chaos

Already in the 1980s, social researchers, Meyer & Zucker (1989), signalled the collapse of the patriarchal system exemplified in the precarious state of several major institutions.

More significantly, they highlighted an inner corrosive decline, whereby certain power-organizations consistently failed to deliver, despite attempts at reform and renewal. The internal malaise, evidenced particularly in the inability to readjust to changing circumstances and in the investment of resources in perpetuating the system itself, became painfully clear in the financial disarray of the first decade of the twenty-first century. Institutional corruption was shown to prevail internationally; for the first time, many people awoke to the bitter truth of what was happening behind the scenes.

Meanwhile, a new development in 2011, known as the Arab Spring offered a semblance of hope for dwindling institutions, as countries like Tunisia, Egypt and Libya toppled long standing dictators. But many of these countries still remain trapped in autocratic regimes. The euphoria is likely to be short-lived.

What the Arab Spring does signify is an emerging global consciousness, desiring more democratic forms of government on a universal scale. This breakthrough is unlikely to transpire without a significant shift in awareness, and a more concerted mobilization of consciousness, firstly to unmask and dislodge the distortions of the past, and, secondly, to dream alternatives to supersede them. The evolutionary lure of our time is certainly shifting consciousness toward more egalitarian ways of being, giving us unprecedented hope for toppling the powers that have been ascendant for far too long. The revolution is already underway, the violent aspects of which are all too obvious in our brutalized world, but on closer observation, the forces for non-violence are gaining credibility and are likely to play a significant role as we move deeper into the twenty-first century.

What role will religion play in this evolutionary breakthrough? Formal religion is so wrapped up in the dynamics of the patriarchal will-to-power; it is unlikely to make a significant contribution to the rise of the new consciousness. At the religious level, the engagement feels shallow, out-of-touch, and invested primarily in ideological self-perpetuation. Paradoxically, as the human species yearns for a new more empowering freedom, millions of people indoctrinated in co-dependent formative influences, turn to fundamentalist religion for wisdom and guidance. For younger people particularly, the new freedom feels daunting, frightening and breeds a cultural type of insecurity. Fundamentalism, whether religious or political, provides a false haven for structure, security and safety – against the "terrorism" of a world perceived to be falling apart.

Empowered by information

The patriarchal will-to-power is still at the forefront in virtually every domain of modern life. Except for one notable exception: *the information explosion*. This is now everybody's domain, as illustrated vividly in Julian Assange's *Wikileaks* scandal in 2011. No longer in the secret care of educated specialists, information flows through a range of channels and portals in our advanced computerized age. Millions have access to information, much of which was beyond human reach just a few decades ago. Social networking connects millions of people beyond national, religious and cultural boundaries. The impact on human consciousness has not been extensively studied but few can deny that this marks a cultural paradigm shift of enormous importance.

What makes it unique is the shift in power, coming from the base up, not from the top down. Those in the know command the high ground, and information is likely to become the greatest social and political catalyst for change as we move further into the twenty-first century. It is likely to paralyze the patriarchal will-to-power and disrupt several power-games that have dominated our landscape for far too long.

A lot of people have yet to be persuaded that our prevailing power-system –whether in politics, economics, social order or religion –is a distortion that has outlived its usefulness. Millions suspect this to be the case, but most have not succeeded in naming it, and such naming is the beginning of a more proactive strategy to unmask and deconstruct the underlying distortion.

4. *When God Rules from the Skyline*

The unquestioned assumption: *God rules from above the sky. He is the one who is in charge and carefully chooses those through whom he will mediate that power.*

If we are to judge by popular media, religion has lost much of its impact in the modern world. Yet, religious coverage is quite extensive in our daily news bulletins. Religious news is often tainted and slanted, with stereotypes that have long outlived their usefulness still dominating the prevailing rhetoric. Among the stereotypes is the divine attribution of an all-powerful God, whose dominance we sometimes deplore, and whose inability (or unwillingness) to act we often bemoan.

Despite several advances in knowledge and wisdom, we still cling to a popular divine stereotype. The majority of religious believers embrace the notion of a God who rules from on high, a male governor whose wisdom is dripped downward through a series of male mediators, some angelic and others human. Paradoxically, non-believers often collude with this projection, thus enhancing the very phenomenon they deem to be so problematic.

The divine right of kings

In the classical cultures of the Middle and Far East, the king came to be seen as the primary representative of God on earth. It is extensively documented in Chinese, Indian, Persian, Greek and Roman mythologies. Kings seem to have evolved for the first time, around 5,000 BCE. Prior to that time, tribal clan leaders were common, but exercised a level of leadership arising from clan or tribal delegation. Going much further back, we trace the role of the Shaman (ness), with a much more specific religious significance. The tribal chief seems to have had more organizational or practical responsibility while the Shaman was the revered spiritual guide within the tribal group.

With the evolution of kingship, several things began to change. The tribal sense of sacredness viewed the divine within creation, not outside it. The divine was understood to be an amorphous, all-pervasive force, embodied in every aspect of what was deemed to be a living creation. Today's indigenous peoples name this divine immanence as the Great Spirit.

The Great Spirit is understood to be an empowering influence, embedded in nature itself, a transformative energy that awakens and releases deeper meaning and creative engagement with the web of life. The Great Spirit is not a person as understood in modern anthropology or in contemporary religion. It is an energetic spirit-force, transcending the personal, yet embracing and endorsing all that is unique to human personhood (more in O'Murchu 2012).

With the evolution of kingship, the sacred shifted from this world to the next, from the immanent creation, deemed to be precarious, prone to sin and temptation, a vale of tears in which one could never find ultimate spiritual fulfillment. And the immanent divine presence, was then transformed into a human-like patriarch, enthroned in a heavenly realm. And from that distant imperial domain, God worked primarily through humans, and only marginally through any other dimension of creation.

Thus, the divine right of kings became the exclusive focus for governance, order, structure and law. God above the sky was the primary royal patron, and mediated his desire for absolute control through the earthly system of kingly governance. In

Christianity the Roman Emperor, Constantine, heavily endorsed this view. Today it dictates almost every feature of the papacy, and continues to heavily infiltrate the hierarchical nature of all Christian denominations.

Our royal loss

With the evolution of kingship and the divine patriarch ruling from beyond the skyline, humans suffered one of the great spiritual losses of all time. The pervasive presence of the Great Spirit was relegated –in time to the point of oblivion. With its suppression, the sacred nature of creation also suffered a cruel displacement. For much of our human evolutionary story, humans lived in deep integration with the living earth itself. Under the kingly dispensation, the close alliance with the earth came to be seen as a primitive form of enmeshment. Instead of being immersed in the natural web of life, the religion-from-on-high required humans (especially men) to distance and separate themselves from this enmeshment. The dualistic split between earth and heaven was sealed, and has prevailed to our own time.

Meanwhile, a more sinister shift had taken place, the negative impact of which still throws a shadow across all modern religions. The *Great Earth Goddess* was violently displaced. Throughout much of the Paleolithic Era (possibly 40,000-10,000 years ago), humans, on an extensive scale, seem to have worshipped God as a Great Mother, embodied primarily in the living earth itself. All that changed with the Agricultural revolution. The Great Mother was replaced with a divine imperial ruler, whose heavenly embodiment belonged to the heavenly realm well beyond this sinful, flawed earth, and whose earthly presence belonged primarily to the ruling King.

God ruled from the Skyline, and never showed his face. He spoke to Moses in a burning bush and to others in pillars of clouds. He communicated with special people through holy emissaries known as angels. And on earth he exercised unilateral control through the male king, who even in parts of the modern world is still deemed to be divine. The perceived role of the pope, the bishop, the Imam, and the synagogue ruler, all adopt this kingly status. It has nothing to do with God, and everything to do with male patriarchal distortion and projection. And it dreads any move that tries to bring God too close to the human and earthly realms.

Power disempowers

In all major religions today, power is a problematic issue. People want to have a say in the running of their church, their synagogue, and their mosque. People want to be involved, to contribute and participate. On the other hand, when structures are provided for greater participation, many do not want to get too close, and it tends to be a minority who opt for greater mutuality and engagement. A strange ambivalence prevails, a psychological residue of the suppression and disempowerment that has prevailed for several centuries, even for a few thousand years.

Nobody wins in this messy inherited landscape. Leaders feel threatened and unsure of their role. People want greater participation yet are reluctant to engage when opportunity comes their way. Inherited wisdom has been discredited on several significant fronts, for instance, the violence so blatantly proclaimed and upheld by scriptures of the monotheistic religions. Truth is open to several interpretations, and the dialogical skills needed for deeper discernment are in scarce supply.

Of particular concern for the religions, and those seeking to protect religious truth, is a double fear: firstly, that the kingly God will be dethroned, but more frightening, that we might expose the shallow foundations upon which the notion of God has been constructed in the first place. Distortions abound when dealing with the God question. Power dominates the landscape, and many attributes we assign to God are actually projections of our own will to dominate and control.

Today, we seem to be on a more authentic ground in striving to discern divine reality (holy mystery) from within the workings of creation itself. When we begin to comprehend the mystery that is our cosmic and planetary creation, we do indeed detect a sense of depth and profundity. This is a new spiritual landscape where we are more likely to encounter what indigenous peoples have long known as the Great Spirit, an enduring and living sense of Holy Mystery. We will pick up the pursuit in Parts Two and Three.

It will take some time to replace the dethroned sovereign ruler! The non-patriarchal structures will take time to evolve, as there are few precedents we can draw upon. There will be attempts at entrenchment, as we currently witness in Roman Catholicism and in the Muslim religion. For those who seek to safeguard religious truth, it will feel as if they are winning the "battle", but what they will often fail to notice is how many reflective followers have moved out and moved away. A new power structure may be in place, and the Skyline God may seem to be in charge once more, but the rank-and-file are not too worried. They have moved on and are seeking something different. What they are seeking becomes clearer in Parts Two and Three of this book.

5. *When Religion Subverted Spirituality*

The unquestioned assumption: *Religion is of God and is essential to exert God-given power and control. The only genuine and authentic spirituality is that which emanates from religion.*

The formal opening of the LHC –the particle collider – at CERN, near Geneva in September 2008, created a flurry of excitement across the planet. Nearly every news channel in the world reported what was happening and in most cases included it among their top headlines. Although millions did not know what exactly was at stake, intuitively and subconsciously people knew that something of great depth and complexity was being explored. In some inexplicable way they believed it was intimately connected with human and earthly life.

On Dec.13, 2011, we experienced another flurry of media excitement, as scientists at CERN confirmed that they were tantalizingly close to nailing the *Higgs Boson*, the particle that would shed light on what gives mass to all other particles, and thus would enable the physicists to pronounce more authoritatively on the make-up of the physical universe. One wonders how many people detected the misguided wisdom, subverted within the excitement of the news release. An estimated 99% of atoms is empty space; the material dimension is a mere 1%. The deeper truth of what the universe is made of will not be revealed through its materiality but by a better understanding of the empty fertile space. Some scientists venture to call such emptiness *consciousness* (Chalmers 1996; van Lommel 2010). Perhaps the search for consciousness should replace the pursuit of the ultimate building blocks!

And one wonders how can anybody come to terms with these awesome questions without a whole new sense of spirituality. These new exploratory horizons have nothing to do with formal religion, in any shape or form, yet people detect something deeply mysterious in these breakthroughs of our time. In 1988, the physicist Stephen Hawking published his best seller *A Brief History of Time*. Even people like me who had no scientific background extensively read it. And I suspect others experienced what I did: I was enthralled by the book although rationally I understood very little of the contents. For many people today, science speaks a powerful spiritual language; it connects us with a spiritual awakening unique to our time, and posing a disturbing challenge for mainline religion today.

Religious worldviews

We have inherited a religious worldview which is still largely taken for granted, assumed to be good, or at least not harmful, when in fact it is causing a great deal of arrested growth and therefore needs to be rectified (if possible) or otherwise abandoned. The religion I know best is Christianity. That which I deem to be defective in our inherited Christian worldview happens to be a kind of dysfunction that prevails in several of major world religions. The world is deemed to be corrupt or sinful, chiefly because humans are. It needs to be rescued (redeemed) and only God can do that in a dramatic salvific plan beyond anything corrupt humans are capable of achieving. In the Judeo-Christian worldview, the action-plan is known as *Restoration Eschatology*.

This is how it has been described in a recent book co-authored by a Christian and Jewish scholar (Madigan & Levenson 2008, 5):

> *Restoration eschatology* arose in large part out of prophetic reaction to the Jewish experience of exile in Babylonia in the sixth century BCE, as well as out of reflection during the postexilic period on the experience of domination by outsiders. The experience of exile and subjugation, fused with the abiding conviction that God would remain true to his covenant, gave rise to the hope expressed classically by the prophets, that God would "restore" Israel, to the Jewish people. Despite present circumstances of exile or subjugation, the prophets affirmed, God would eventually establish his reign or kingdom. The forces dominating, frustrating, often even polluting or provoking Israel would ultimately and definitively be overthrown. The God of Israel would reclaim his throne, his capital city Jerusalem would be restored, and his palace, the temple, rebuilt. The lost tribes would also be "gathered back in." The dead would rise and all would be judged by God. . . .God would make a new creation to vindicate his loyal people.

This dominant myth –another inherited distortion - can be detected in most, if not all, of the major world religions. These are some of the key elements:

a) Creation is flawed and humans are disobedient to God; on closer examination it is humans who are flawed and therefore creation is also perceived to be innately corruptible. A defective anthropology is at the root of the problem.

b) The sense of exile being described suggests that humans are fundamentally at variance with God. In fact, the cause of the exile (or alienation) arises from a faulty relationship with the surrounding creation, and not with God.

c) The relationship with creation is dysfunctional because the cosmology being employed is suffocating and perverse; all creation is subsumed into one tiny sector of planet Earth, in this case the state of Israel.

d) Consequently, the God-image being used is that of a nationalistic, patriarchal (king-like) hero who exerts control through violence, adopting the patriarchal ploy of divide-and-conquer.

e) Violence becomes an integral dimension of formal religion, with God primarily on the side of the winner, not the loser. The loser can only be saved by divine rescue, an initiative totally in God's hands. (See the informed critique of Sam Harris 2005).

f) Dualistic splitting dominates the entire landscape. God is active, humans passive; God is good, humans sinful. Only religion can bridge the chasm, and can only do so fully in a life hereafter.

Enter spirituality . . .

Throughout the closing decades of the twentieth century, spirituality came into fashion as an alternative viewpoint on the meaning and purpose of religion. It continues to enjoy wide popularity, setting forth a number of correctives to the dominant religious worldview:

> a) God works primarily through creation, not merely through humans. Creation in its entire cosmic and planetary dimensions needs to be reclaimed as the primary manifestation (revelation) of what God is and how God works among us.

> b) Like everything else in God's creation, humans are evolving creatures, called to be co-creators with our creative God. Instead of focusing on limitations (sin) as religion does, we need to embrace in a more conscious way our graced potentials for our God-given responsibilities.

> c) This is what humans seem to have achieved for most of our seven million year story on this earth, a primordial empowering story that has been short-circuited and demonized by formal religion.

> d) The long story indicates that humans behave more constructively and creatively when we remain very close to nature. It is our violent disassociation from the natural world (encouraged by religion) that is at the root of the many violent problems confronting humanity today.

> e) Salvation/redemption is a human responsibility, when people re-awaken to their call to be co-creators and consciously adopt attitudes and behaviors to co-create with the living Spirit which inhabits everything in creation.

f) While religion flourishes on cultural co-dependency (keeping people dependent and child-like), spirituality aims to re-awaken and empower afresh adult people mutually relating with an adult God.

BOX: Distinguishing Features of Religion and Spirituality

RELIGION	SPIRITUALITY
Culturally validated creedal systems	An enlarged inner sense of the sacred
Based on revealed Scriptures	Based on a search for new meaning
Publicly acknowledged dogmas	A fluid and evolving sense of truth
An ethical code	Veers towards situational ethics
A system of public worship	Spontaneous, flexible rituals.
Focus: escape to the world beyond	Focus: engagement with creation
Hierarchical leadership	Egalitarian and often individualistic
Strongly human-centered	Often trans-human, ecological & cosmic
Tendency towards dualisms	Strongly holistic

A difficult transition

Despite vociferous voices denouncing religion as regressive and infantile, religious fervor is more than holding its own. In fact, closer investigation would probably show that it is on the increase. What is increasing, however, is not religion as a cultural artifact – providing society with official sacred text (scripture), a moral code, and formal guidelines for worship – but a more formless, vaguely defined religiosity (spirituality), with positive and negative elements.

You can pick and choose from these negative features that tend to be highlighted in scholarly research: individualistic, postmodernist, incestuous, recklessly dispensing with tradition, idolatrous, more secular than sacred. Many of these elements can be understood as a reaction to an earlier rigidity and dogmatism that stripped religious fervor of joy and spontaneity, and often inhibited the creative freedom of the Spirit in religious rite and expression.

What is newly emerging may require a new language to comprehend its cultural impact. Hence, the popularity of the word, *spirituality*, to describe what is evolving at this time. As I shall indicate later in this book, this new spirituality is not merely a novel attempt at engaging the sacred in our lives, but subconsciously, it also seeks to reclaim a spiritual orientation known to humans long before formal religion evolved (about 5,000 years ago). In this sense, spirituality denotes a paradigm shift of great age, with cultural implications that are unlikely to be honored within the context of religion, as we understand it today.

6. *The Myth of the Hunting Males*

The unquestioned assumption: *By nature men are hunters and have been so since time immemorial. Competition, and at times violence, is necessary for evolution and for human survival.*

In 2005, Robert Sussman of Washington University in St. Louis (USA), and his one-time undergraduate student, Donna Hart, published the fruit of some masterly research in a book entitled *Man the Hunted* (Hart & Sussman 2005). Most of the book is devoted to the human struggle over many millennia to defend humans against the super power and skill of wild animals and their ability to subdue and kill humans. For most of our evolutionary history we have been hunted, long before we began to hunt.

More significantly, Hart and Sussman challenge the largely unquestioned assumption that we have been hunters for a long time and that the practice of hunting dictates many of our social and cultural customs today. The evidence for this claim is quite superficial, based on cultural projections rather than informed research. Hart and Sussman conclude that prior to 500,000 years ago (out of an evolutionary story of seven million years) there is scant evidence for the myth of the hunting male. For most of our time, we were horticultural food-gatherers rather than meat-hunters.

Cultural projections

The projections go along these lines: if humans today are violent and competitive as indeed we are, then our ancient ancestors must have been much worse, because allegedly we have improved over time (a fallacious worldview). And this tendency for males to dominate, and do so violently at times, can be traced back to our hunting behavior, assumed to be as old as humanity itself – reinforced by the perception that meat-eating is essential to our physical growth and human development.

A further nuance to these perceptions is the assumption that the further back we go in time, the more we behaved like animals who also compete and at times cannibalize. As we left behind us the wild and violent animal, as we differentiated into more civilized creatures – in the past five to ten thousand years – we gradually abandoned the ferocious nature of the violent hunter. (In this argument we conveniently ignore how we are translating the repressed violence into warfare and the several other forms of violence so endemic to our time).

Anthropologists are shifting the attention to our horticultural status whereby we foraged for food, long before we killed for meat. For much of our evolutionary history we were vegetarians rather than meat-eaters. And even when we did hunt for meat, roots, berries and vegetables still remained the core ingredients of our stable diet.

Scholars are also noting the social and ritualistic significance of the hunt. As the spirit of competition began to surface, among males particularly, the chasing, seizing and killing of the animal was an achievement meriting recognition, status and priority in the tribe. It may also have resulted in acquiring sexual favor, as one brought home meat for the sustenance of the family.

The extensive use of animal depictions in the Ice Age Art caves suggests that animals had an honored place in ancient rituals. We should not quickly conclude that the sacrifice of animals to placate the Gods has ancient roots because in fact the evidence for this practice does not seem as old and extensive as many think. Nonetheless, the killing of the animal in prehistoric cultures certainly had spiritual significance, and is likely to have been done with a good deal of care and even devotion.

The hunting myth

At a subtle, but pervasive level, the hunting myth underpins our prevailing worldview, and reinforces several of the cultural distortions I am seeking to name and unmask in the first Part of this book. The male as wage-earner, as the one who has the right to dominate and control, the patriarchal head of the family, the one more suited for hard manual tasks, all can be traced to the cult of the ancient hunt. It also fuels a great deal of the fierce competition that characterizes almost every form of sport in the modern world.

Much more problematic is our addiction to violence, overtly manifest in warfare and the several conflicts that characterize our world today, but covertly insinuated into the violence that features so strongly in the media and the arts. *Lord of the Rings* hit international fame in the opening decade of the twenty-first century, but few commentators drew attention to the extensive violence exhibited throughout the movie. By the same token, we tend to censor TV shows for anything relating to explicit sexual behavior but tolerate a substantial amount of gory, brutal imagery, much of which creates a lurid fascination for naïve viewers. It is suggested that we need this bombardment of media violence as a cathartic release for the hunter instinct that is endemic to all of us.

It also impacts heavily on how we understand and appropriate human sexuality. Sexuality is widely perceived as having one basic function: the procreation of the species. In other words, sexuality is deemed to be a mechanism for biological reproduction and up till the twentieth century it was widely assumed that the male seed plays the major role in the reproductive process. In Africa, many rites of initiation focus primarily on the male, and the need to reinforce male prowess. Despite a great deal of attention to the female body in advertising and commercialization, it is the satisfaction of male libido that dictates the surreal process of sensation and stimulation. The male drive dictates and controls the sexualization of culture - as perceptively noted by the French philosopher, Michel Foucault, in his oft-cited three-volume work on sexuality as an instrument of power.

Our violent instinct

As a species we collude heavily with the culture of violence. We validate it in the name of an aggressive inheritance considered to be as old as humanity itself. We postulate its essential nature on the assumption that animals and primates are innately violent, a viewpoint challenged by several researchers in recent decades most notably by Jane Goodall. More subtly still, we sanction violence in the name of a divine ruler who defeats his enemies and supports those who kill and maim to safeguard religious orthodoxy.

In our patriarchal cultures there is a deeply embedded reluctance to look too closely at the rationale whereby we tolerate and justify violence. If we look too closely, we might have to re-examine the competitive drive upon which so much political and economic prowess is based. Then, the entire cultural canopy of our modern world might be in jeopardy, and those that enjoy the privilege of power might be seriously disenfranchised.

In the opening decade of the twenty-first century a number of significant publications highlight that humans are programmed primarily for cooperation, and not for competition (De Waal 2010; Keltner & Alia 2010; Rifkin 2009). The claim is not entirely new; in fact, this collaborative strain belongs to a bedrock understanding of how we flourished and thrived as an evolutionary species (more in O'Murchu 2009). But with the virulent hunting male, still so deeply ingrained in our collective psyche, it will take time to embrace more overtly these new insights and the major implications for a different way of living. It feels like a paradigm shift almost too big to embrace.

Our violent cultural projections

The twentieth century has been described as the most violent of all time. (http://www.scaruffi.com/politics/massacre. html; http://necrometrics.com/20c5m.htm). An estimated 250 million people were massacred in warfare around the world, and that figure merely represents the formal records. As is widely known, the deadly toll on civilians and innocent people is rarely recorded; it far exceeds what is detailed in the formal accounts. And in the opening decades of the twenty-first century, the violence continues unabated – with an average of three million war casualties each year since the turn of the century. Whether it be the travesty of warfare, the conflict of tribal divisions, the barbarity of street crime, the apparent disregard for human life, the atrocious suffering imposed upon animal and plant life each day, the often barbaric exploitation of the living earth itself, the cruelty continues unabated!

We have created a human project that would seem to fall apart without violence. Conflict and destruction have become innate to our way of dealing with reality, inwardly and outwardly. Our economics and politics, international trade and sophisticated advertising, our mass media, and the entertainment industry, all seem to need violence as a driving force.

The assumption that war is necessary to preserve some semblance of peace in the world, is one of the most serious and convoluted distortions of our inherited patriarchal worldview. The underlying distortion is rarely acknowledged, namely that the politics of patriarchy are fundamentally adversarial, conflictual, and prone to create antagonism and division. It is not our animal instincts that cause the problem. The source is much more subtle and deep-seated. And having been religiously validated for so many centuries – in the divine right of Kings to serve and appease a violent Deity – there prevails a deep-seated cultural resistance to name and expose the deeper causes.

Violence is a human product –more specially a patriarchal male malfunction. Like the many other cultural distortions named in this book, it can only be challenged after we have first named and unmasked the underlying energy-force. In doing so, we are going to encounter fierce resistance, and we will be ridiculed and scapegoated. So much in our prevailing culture –including our economics – is based on retaining a culture of violence and warfare. It will not be an easy conversion, but one we must face and confront, if we stand any hope of a habitable planet for the foreseeable future.

$$\approx \diamondsuit \approx$$

7. *Economics based on Scarcity*

The unquestioned assumption: *There are only limited resources on the planet, and to access the resources fairly we need market strategies that will encourage people to compete for the scarce goods, and let the invisible hand of the market guide the process.*

In an influential 1932 essay, Lionel Robbins defined economics as "the science which studies human behavior as a relationship between ends and scarce means which have alternative uses."

The concept of *scarcity* is essential to the field of economics. A resource is considered scarce when its availability is not enough to meet its demand. Scarcity is based on the idea that oftentimes a limited supply of goods or services comes up against an ever-increasing demand for it; therefore, every effort must be made to ensure its proper utilization and distribution so as to avoid inefficiency. Most goods and services can be defined as scarce since individuals desire more of them than they already possess. Scarcity is maintained by demand. Those that are readily abundant are referred to as free goods.

The scarcity of goods and services is brought about by factors such as the limited supply of resources, for example, water, land or people; and the limited capabilities of technology or human skill, for example, those needed for enhanced production. Sometimes the insufficiencies are a result of poor planning and execution. In such cases, the scarcity is considered artificial.

Scarcity is managed by making choices regarding value so that individuals can exchange resources in a system of trade. In ideal circumstances, pricing systems adjust accordingly, thereby maintaining the balance of supply and demand. Certain things require scarcity to maintain value, as is the case, for example, with diamonds, awards, even the money produced by central banks.

Unmasking the rhetoric

There is a dangerous and sinister camouflage in this economic theory, and it was unmasked in September 2008, when the United States government suggested a 700 billion dollar bailout for failing (or failed?) economic institutions in their country. Among rank-and-file folks the anger was visible as thousands realized that the institutions to which they entrusted their money and financial security had been recklessly trading their trust and resources. And instead of calling the institutions to accountability and transparency, the taxpayers of the nation were being asked to fund the bailout.

In other words, the largely unregulated market had run amok. The sarcastically described "fat cats" had squandered millions of dollars. If the taxpayer had no one to bail him/her out – which is often the case when facing unmet mortgage payments – why should the taxpayer be burdened with the ordeal of salvaging the irresponsible institutions? Of course many now know the answer to that question but dread the thought of contemplating it too deeply: *because the entire economic system is essentially corrupt and dysfunctional.*

The collusion between the economic system and mainstream government contributes to the internal corruption, with extensive personal dislocation, social disruption and ecological breakdown on a massive scale. The fragile foundation of the entire system becomes even more precarious when we realize that money today is held and filtered primarily by transnational corporations and not by nation-based banking systems. This leaves the human individual perplexed, vulnerable and almost totally at a loss on where to turn for trustworthy advice. It becomes all too clear on where future hope rests - return the entire system to local initiative. One wonders how bad will things need to become before humans begin to reclaim money for the "local commons" (more in Eisenstien 2011) where it had its historical origins and where it will activate the greatest sense of empowerment for humans and earth-life alike.

The greatest lie of all

The prevailing economic system is based on one big lie: *the scarcity of resources.* We inhabit a universe of *abundance*, not of scarcity. On planet Earth, we are blessed with an abundant supply that can sustain and nourish billions of creatures, human and non-human alike, provided we adopt a system of fair and just distribution, informed by the values of sustainability and economic transparency.

The capitalistic value-system is a consequence of the patriarchal worldview we briefly reviewed in the opening chapters of this book. Money is a commodity that thrives when we regard everything else as mere objects, including human beings. This happens when humans objectify the goods of the earth into resources that are to be used to benefit them in a laissez-faire market system; the strong and clever (devious) ones win and everybody else loses out. But instead of describing the process in terms of brutal power-games, those who monopolize the resources argue that the goods are scarce and therefore require this extensive exploitation to access the scarce supply of goods.

The hard sell is incredibly seductive, devious and sinister. It now adopts a repertoire of modern knowledge and technology to exploit even further a consumer culture becoming more and more petrified as the economic paradigm itself progressively fragments. One recent author, Chris Anderson (2006), outlines the luring benefits of the digital market. Rabid, glitzy advertising, attracting gullible consumers, for online convenience shopping, is likely to dominate the economic scene for the foreseeable future. It gives the impression of freedom, flexibility and empowerment, when in fact it is another – more devious – form of economic and political manipulation.

The money crisis

The precarious financial state of our world today is not based on a shortage of money, or on the gold reserves to back up the money. The crisis arises from a prolonged distortion relating to the very meaning of money itself. As Thomas Greco (2009) indicates, economics was never meant to be a science at variance with people's genuine needs and the organic needs of the living Earth itself; it was meant to serve those needs, and empower people to engage in social and economic activity that would empower rather than undermine creative affiliation with the cosmic web of life. More recently, the American philosopher, Charles Eisenstein (2011) offers a more penetrating critique, pointing out that it is the betrayal of the fundamental nature of money as a mechanism for *mutual gifting*, that has launched us in the economic mess in which we find ourselves; how to reclaim this foundational significance is outlined in Part Three.

Eistenstein further illuminates the convoluted nature of the current crisis. We set up a competitive functional arrangement (markets) to deal with the scarcity. Within that strategy we began multiplying supplies of money itself, and there was never enough. This led to an accumulation of debt, which itself grew in exponential proportions. Internationally, we now employ a vastly complex and cumbersome economic system *to pay off debt*. It is the unceasing payment of debts that is fuelling our current economic system. Debt is at the heart of economic crisis. In Greco's words (2009, 62):

> Virtually all the money throughout the world today is created by banks as debt… the banking system today causes a debt imperative, which drives a growth imperative – this forces destructive competition for the available supply of money, which is never sufficient to enable all debtors to pay what they owe.

The economist, Michael Hudson (quoted in Greco 2009, 64) adds an alarming prognostication: "The economy has reached its debt-limit and is entering its insolvency phase. We are not in a cycle but the end of an era. The old world of debt pyramiding to a fraudulent degree cannot be restored."

The brief reflections of this section translate into a clarion call to the human species: *wake up and face the demise staring us in the face.* The allurement of wealth and the seductive trap of money-making (more accurately, of debt-accumulation) are rapidly reaching unsustainable levels. Neither governments nor banks are acting with either transparency or propriety. They are locked into a complicit collusion from which they cannot extricate themselves, never mind empower the general public.

We need to wake up to the chaotic financial mess in which we are all implicated. And having become aware, then we can begin the long and arduous task to re-imagine a more empowering and enriching economic system. Fortunately, creative minds are already at work. The outline of an alternative financial system has already received considerable attention, and some promising alternatives have been tried and tested. However, the quantum leap now urgently needed is unlikely to happen, till many more people register their disapproval of the current practice, and shift their creative imaginations to the reconstruction of a more hopeful future. We'll pick it up from there in Part Three.

8. *The Politics of Commodification*

The unquestioned assumption: *Political structures, such as the Nation State and mega-corporations are essential to the patriarchal task of divide and conquer*

The science of politics was first drawn up in classical Greek times, predominantly by Plato and Aristotle. The Greek *polis* (city) denoted the assembled body of eminent citizens who helped to regulate and organize social life on behalf of the people. At the heart of the organization, however, was the King, not merely an earthly imperial ruler, but also widely acknowledged as the primary representative on earth of the God who rules from above the sky. Politics, in its classical origins, was the handmaid of religion. It was the same patriarchal God figure who guided both. The distinction between the sacred and the secular, between Church and State, was unknown before the Christian era.

All patriarchal societies are characterized by a system of male kinship in which men are counted as kin because they are descended from the same male ancestor. Paternal authority is the ruling principle of the social order. In ancient Rome, the *pater potestas* extended to all descendants of one living male ancestor; it comprised control and punishment, not to mention questions of life and death.

The Nation State

Today, human governance, which is still unmistakably patriarchal, is facilitated officially through the Nation State, a political unit envisaged in ancient Greek times, and promoted in Roman times. But it is a structure that did not assume its current significance until the seventeenth century in Europe – after the Peace of Westphalia in 1648. It is often suggested that the origin of the state is to be found in the development of the art of warfare. All political communities of the modern type owe their existence to successful warfare. As a result the new states are forced to organize on military principles. Several nation states evolved out of what was initially a military alliance.

Of the systems of government adopted for state management, that of kingship stands to the fore, until the French Revolution put an end to the "divine right of kings" in Europe, a divine prerogative which lasted longer in other regions, particularly in the Far East. In most premodern cultures, the State was just a territory ruled by a king who was surrounded by a small elite group of warriors and court officials. It basically ruled by force over a larger mass of people. Slowly, however, the people gained political representation and towards the end of the nineteenth century more democratic systems began to evolve, with elected governments delegated to facilitate financial, legal, and social transactions to the benefit of the masses.

Nationalism in jeopardy

Today, it is widely assumed that the Nation State is the most effective and reliable instrument of governance. Millions do not seem to be aware of the violent military background that led to the formation of many contemporary states, nor do most people realize the very artificial and problematic borders that surround most states. Much more serious, is the usurpation of the Nation State by the forces of globalization throughout the closing decades of the twentieth century. Today, several major political and economic decisions are not dictated by nation states but by transnational corporations. Most of the wealth is in the hands of corporations. Several patents (copyright) on essential goods (e.g., cocoa from Ghana, vanilla from Madagascar) are held by corporations who under WTO law have the right to override decisions made by national governments.

Control by a minority over the majority is the rationale of both nation states and transnational corporations. Democracy is a veneer to which millions of gullible people submit. In national elections we choose our government representatives, but for the duration of their commission (4-6 years) we have little or no say on what transpires within the procedures of governance. Modern democratic posturing is a camouflaged application of the older more overt patriarchal philosophy of divide-and-conquer.

As we enter the twenty-first century, a progressive corrosion characterizes our dominant ways of doing governance. Increasing numbers of people have become cynical and disillusioned. Many acknowledge that the system is breaking down and no longer seems capable of serving our true needs. We have been so conditioned and controlled, over a long period of time, that people struggle to imagine alternatives to the prevailing system. It is sometimes suggested that the dysfunctionality of the prevailing system needs to become more unworkable before people will veer towards possible alternatives with more coherent vision and consistent commitment. What those alternatives might look like is explored in Part Three of this book.

Debilitating disempowerment

Political fatalism is rampant in the contemporary world. Firstly, there are the millions condemned to poverty and daily degradation. The focus of attention is the day-to-day survival. They eke out a meager existence from the limited resources they claim to own, or share with a range of others. Researchers often glamorize the apparent happiness of these people living on next-to-nothing. They have no choice but to be "happy" because if they were to take seriously the nature of their plight they would quickly succumb to total despair. The only political governance such people know is occasional interference of the big chief, often a tribal ruler, called on to sort out a situation of social conflict.

A few steps further up the social ladder are another sector of humanity comprising millions as well. They are destitute and poor, often devastated by floods or storms. However they have a minimal education system and thanks to the initiative of NGOs a sense of the larger world, which they perceive as largely indifferent to their plight unless it can rob them of some lucrative resources, mineral or otherwise. Several African nations fit into this category, as does countries in Asia like the Philippines, Laos and Burma (Mynmar).

Next on the hierarchy we review the average low-wage citizenry, whether in the West or elsewhere. Such people are lured by the prospect of being able to cast a vote and select a government. Occasionally, they will benefit from a hand-me-down that will keep them quiet and collusive with the system, which at the end of the day has little or no interest in their welfare. Millions also belong to this category, and thanks to the growing awareness percolating their ranks (via information), they are becoming more cynical towards political and economic systems and becoming more disillusioned by the corruption of power which they are beginning to understand with clearer insight.

Towards the top of the ladder, are the well-do-do, whether financially or socially. They trust government as long as they benefit from it economically, and they can retain a semblance of sanity by being able to participate in the merry-go-round of financial exploitation. They comprise no more than 10% of the entire human race.

It is a grim and rather frightening picture – the several embedded distortions that defy all sense of credibility. How could any species have ever allowed such an outrageous aberration to gain such cultural supremacy? In political terms, the vast majority has been condemned to debilitating disempowerment. And most people have been so effectively indoctrinated that they are not even aware of the deplorable plight into which we have plunged ourselves.

It is highly unlikely that we can redeem this system. Who wants to redeem it anyhow? Perhaps, the most responsible action is to withdraw energy from it – simply do not collude with it in order to bring it to its knees! This is considered a recklessly subversive suggestion, but in times of bewildering change we are often forced to embrace drastic choices. And we do need to learn to reserve energy for what has prospects of a more hopeful future – the features of which are outlined in Part Three of this book.

In reading the signs of the times, we must strive to be honest and transparent in how we perceive and name our encompassing reality. That, in itself, gives some semblance of hope. The grim picture of this section is an attempt at such honesty, in the belief that ultimately the truth will set us free. Hopefully it will free us up to place our energy where it is likely to make a more constructive difference.

9. *Advertising the Surreal*

The unquestioned assumption: *Because the market is essentially competitive we must devise sales strategies and techniques to convert people into being good consumers. Slick advertising is the way to do it.*

Now we come to what may be the most devious distortion of all: *advertising*! This is how the cultural indoctrination takes place. And it becomes ever more subtle, devious, alluring and irresistible.

Every day, from birth to death, we are bombarded with salacious, seductive imagery. Human desiring has been infiltrated, and distorted to such an extent that we can no longer differentiate truth from falsity, fact from fiction, substance from superficiality. More precisely, the mental faculties through which we make such discriminations are so driven, corrupted and addicted, that we are unable to mobilize the more rational side of ourselves to do the things we know we ought to do. We have been captivated by seductive images and the compulsive urge to seek more and more gratification. It quickly comes to a stage where enough is never enough!

Guerrilla advertising

A recent advertising innovation known as "guerrilla marketing", involves unusual approaches such as staged encounters in public places, giveaways of products such as cars that are covered with brand messages, and interactive advertising where the viewer can respond to become part of the advertising message. Guerrilla advertising is becoming increasingly more popular with a lot of companies. It has adopted up-to-the-minute technology such as texting and social networking. With minimum effort the consumer is lured into purchasing an array of products one does not really need at all. And even those living off limited financial means are pressurized to be as good as everybody else, and crave the popular products that are of little or no benefit. In fact, they often plunge people into further debt and poverty.

Semiotics is the study of signs and how they are interpreted. Today's culture uses sophisticated means to sensationalize the human imagination, and distort it into seeking a fleeting happiness with the promise of the market that it will fulfill every human need. Advertising has many hidden signs and meanings within brand names, logos, package designs, print advertisements, and television advertisements. The purpose of semiotics is to study and interpret the message being conveyed in advertisements.

The researchers –sometimes indoctrinated themselves through their "professional"training –interpret advertising at two layers, known as the surface level and the underlying level. The surface level uses signs creatively to reproduce an image or personality for their product. These signs can be images, words, fonts, colors, or slogans. The underlying level is made up of the hidden meanings, and it is at this stage that the indoctrination has the greatest impact.

The Apple computer company is an excellent example of using semiotics in its advertising campaign. Apple's commercials used a black silhouette of a person, placing it in front of a blue screen so that the picture behind the silhouette could be constantly changing. However, the one thing that stays the same in these ads is that there is music in the background and the silhouette is listening to that music on a white iPod through white headphones. Through advertising, the white color on a set of earphones now signifies that the music device is an iPod. The white color signifies almost all of Apple's products.

The semiotics of gender plays a key influence on the way in which signs are interpreted. Research suggests that males tend to respond better to objective marketing, external descriptions and factual information, whereas females tend to respond better to subjective claims that evoke emotional stimulation. Men prefer to have available and apparent cues to interpret the message where females engage in more creative, associative, imagery-laced interpretations. Most voice-overs are men (figures of up to 94% have been reported). There have been more female voice-overs in recent years but mainly for food, household products, and feminine care products.

Indoctrination of youth

It is youth and children that are most intensely subjected to the psychological power of advertising. It is at increasingly younger ages that the seeds of life-long indoctrination are sown. According to an American study conducted in 1999: marketing expert James U. McNeal, PhD, (author of *The Kids Market: Myths and Realities,* Paramount Market Publishing, 1999), highlights that advertising induces children under 12 to spend a whopping $28 billion a year. Teenagers spend $100 billion. Children also influence another $249 billion spent by their parents.

A recent national survey found the average child in the United States spends six and a half hours a day using various forms of media. This is more than any other activity done while awake. The majority of this time is spent watching television. The average American child will see more than 40,000 television commercials every year, in addition to seeing product placement in all different media outlets.

Much more disturbing –and reinforcing the distortion under consideration –is the manipulation of our educational systems in favor of the values of capitalism. From a young age we indoctrinate our children to be fierce competitors, socially and academically. In this process, we encourage and reward our youth for colluding with the market-orientation of the dominant culture. Thus our young people are not educated into being critical thinkers, who will reflect more discriminately and challenge the prevailing cultural values. They are uncritically absorbed into the hard-sell advertising, and as indicated above, they are often the catalysts for their parents – and even their teachers – to become more amenable to the influence of advertising propaganda.

Education's failure

In the contemporary world we fail to distinguish between *information, knowledge,* and *wisdom.* First of all, we live in an information age, which certainly is empowering for the masses, enabling people to access global information through a range of technological outlets. This is rapidly becoming a global phenomenon, even in poorer countries. However, the empowerment is of questionable worth, since most people seem poorly skilled on how to differentiate between useful and useless information, constructive and destructive forms. The information explosion feeds even more virulently the seductive advertising that has captured the mind and spirit of so many people.

Secondly, there is knowledge, what philosophers of earlier times called *scientia*. It is the know-how that skills and empowers us to live and act intelligently in the world. However, knowledge has also been usurped by power mongering, and now has been sequestered mainly by academic institutions. Thus the universities provide the experts that will advise governments and corporations. In most cases, such advice becomes an endorsement of the mindset of the status quo. Frequently, people's real needs are overseen amid the plethora of theories and recommendations.

Thus knowledge has become a kind of handmaid of patriarchal power, elevating academic achievement to an elite status. The boundary between the academic and intellectual is blurred, giving pride of place to the academic. We are all blessed with the gift of intellect, and millions who have no academic achievements —no letters to display after their names —are nonetheless insightful and innovative, often in more practical and empowering ways than the academics.

This brings me to the third category: *wisdom*. In the modern world this is the big loser, another tragic consequence of the distortion under consideration in this Section. According to the Christian teaching, the wise shall inherit the earth. Not while we pursue business as usual in the modern world! There is no space – nor is there any welcome - for indigenous, ground-up wisdom in our contemporary age. Indigenous peoples struggle to maintain some semblance of innate wisdom, and where endorsed, is a meager effort; and that too is sometimes sequestered to support the mainline culture.

Cultural catalysts

When it comes to the inculcation of an empowering wisdom, educational systems all over our planet have proved to be a dismal failure. The knowledge transmitted tends to be functional, and favors those who compete more effectively. Information bombards us from every side. People – both young and elderly – are poorly equipped with the skills necessary for good discrimination. The acquisition of wisdom, in so far as it happens, arises from life-experience, among those critical and innovative enough to ask more discerning questions, and opt for counter-cultural possibilities.

The cultural catalysts of our time are certainly on the increase. However, it will take at least a number of decades to create the alternative consciousness to undo (or at least soften) the fierce grip that advertising has on the human imagination at this time. So many people are duped into superficiality, seduced by the glitzy advertising that bombards our senses daily.

We become what we read, because we have not acquired the skills to read with a more perceptive and critical mind. We also easily succumb to the propaganda of the market requiring us to desire what apparently everybody else wants (or already has), when in truth we are only aggravating our senses to ever more addictive levels. Increasingly our senses become more demanding and impossible to satisfy. Thus we create what Bruce Wilshire (1998) identifies as a wild hunger, the basis of several compulsive behaviors in our time.

We need to make do with less, and learn the value to living within sustainable limits. It enhances our own happiness and fulfilment and is a more congenial way to live as planetary beings. It is easy to state it on paper; to live it out in real life is a tough struggle with so many odds pitched against us.

To become cultural catalysts who can confront the myopia of so much wild destructive propaganda, we need to become more alert and aware. We need to explore as well networks of kindred spirits to help us build up a counter-culture that is conducive to increased social awareness and the exercise of a more responsible purchasing activity. Thus we can begin to challenge the cultural distortion of compulsive advertising and the unhealthy consumerism that follows in its wake.

Second Benchmark: *From Distortions to Transitions*

W hether the reader agrees or disagrees with this brief analysis of our inherited cultural distortions, few can deny their impact upon our daily lives. However, the consciousness of that impact varies enormously. For most people on the planet today, life is about survival. It is about making ends meet, ensuring that there is enough food for daily need, and struggling to support and promote the well-being of loved ones with the meager resources available.

It is a shocking indictment that the majority of human beings have to live like this. In itself it highlights the abysmal failure of the civilized world to deliver anything resembling freedom and empowerment. Our economics, politics, social policies and religions all stand accused of negligence, exploitation and power mongering to reinforce their own dominance and self-inflation. Human beings have been betrayed, and so has the earth, with its resources, and the many other creatures with whom we share the living planet.

So, what do we do about it? Where do we even begin? I suggest we need to start with the foundational issue of the quality and quantity of *our awareness*. We live in a cauldron of appalling ignorance. Buddhism refers to it as illusion, the delusory sense of deception and camouflage whereby most people do not know what is actually going on, and worst still, millions don't want to know.

The poor of the world don't want to know because all their energy goes into the struggle to survive. The rich and powerful don't want to know because it would disturb their need to cling on to their self-inflated worldview. We look to those in between to offer some hope for the future.

Who are these folks? Social historians frequently allude to *consciousness-shifters* and name them in different but related ways. I find the research of the sociologist, Pitrim Sorokin (1957), to be particularly insightful and persuasive on this matter. He claims that in times of cultural change it is *the restless middle classes* who most effectively negotiate the paradigm shifts. They are restless about the plight of the poor and desire to have it changed. They are disgusted with the hoarding and power mongering of the rich (even though they may have benefited from it), and will raise the voice of protest. This may translate into different voting patterns, industrial strike action, protests of various types, or proactive networking - one of the more effective catalytic shifters in our time to which I give much attention throughout this book.

Many of the distortions highlighted above are systemic in nature and have survived for quite some time. Patriarchal institutions contain a strong urge for self-survival and are highly skilled at subverting, demonizing and suppressing social critique, from both within and without. And in the face of radical change, they tend to become deeply entrenched, thus paving the way to become "permanently failing institutions". Several major religions and churches seem to be at this stage of cultural decline.

Becoming more aware

Awareness, therefore, is the first crucial resource to deal proactively with the distortions. If I don'trecognize the flaw, and become more aware of what is really going on, then I am not likely to do something about it. And when, enough people become aware, we stand a better chance of creating the transforming resonance that can help to catalyze effective change. Indeed, we can draw courage from the fact that this threshold of consciousness has evolved significantly in recent decades, thanks particularly to the information explosion.

As we become more aware, the complexity of the major issues in our time becomes all too transparent. Some will throw up their hands in despair at the thought that they can do nothing to bring about change. Others will become angry and even violent, and in the contemporary world, we see abundant evidence for this. And others –particularly those with an empowering spirituality –begin to realize that they cannot do it on their own. They need others. Above all they need systemic empowerment to confront and dislodge the systemic disempowerment. They need to join a network!

Networking, more than any other proactive strategy, offers hope for the future. Networks like Greenpeace, Friends of the Earth, Amnesty International, and many others identified by researchers such as Paul Hawken (2007), are confronting and changing the distortions outlined above. More importantly, they are birthing alternative ways of being, acting and living – paving the way for a different and better future, the ingredients of which I explore in the subsequent sections of this book.

Befriending the chaos

I am suggesting that awareness is a first crucial recourse; the second is the resilience to befriend the chaos of our time in a more consciously proactive way. In other words, let's not succumb to the denial that is rampant in our modern world and contributes directly and indirectly to the paralysis millions of our contemporaries feel.

Disintegration is happening all around us, and the more it surfaces the more desperately our major institutions try to keep it invisible while deluding us with the panacea of business as usual. It is a cruel trick that paralyzes our creativity and subverts our imaginations. Without this breakdown, the disintegration of the old order, there can be no release of fresh energy to engender a novel future. We cannot escape the breakdown. We will only survive it *by going through it*. And the more transparently we can do that the better for all life forms on earth, ourselves included.

In Part Two of this book I am inviting the reader to come out of the shadow of resistant denial, and unmask issues around which we must learn to muster new skills and resilience for greater truth and transparency. We strive to acknowledge chaos and not deny its prevalence. It will not consume us. From our deep past as a species - with a life-story of some seven million years - we have internalized coping mechanisms far more empowering than most of us realize.

In learning to befriend the chaos, we become more grounded in our earthiness and in our embodied selves. We become more real, honest and truthful. And we learn to let-go of old securities no longer useful for our evolutionary emergence. Thus we are made free to be open to the new, and more adventurous and courageous in exploring the novel future into which life is inviting us.

Dealing authentically with chaos comes easy to none of us, but that very process of engagement engenders its own momentum and empowerment. Striving to deal truthfully with reality, beyond the protective confines of our denial, at some stage will lead to a greater freedom, and enhanced skills for creativity. Hopefully, the reflections of Part Two – complex and bewildering at times – will empower us for a deeper and more authentic engagement with the evolutionary changes happening all around us at this time of major cultural change.

$\approx \diamond \approx$

Part Two:

MAKING SENSE OF CREATIVE CHAOS

Life spirals laboriously upward to higher and even higher levels, paying for every step. Death was the price of the multi-cellular condition; pain the price of nervous integration; anxiety the price of consciousness.

Ludwig von Bertalanffy.

When you act on behalf of something greater than yourself, you begin to feel it acting through you with a power that is greater than your own.

Joanna Macy

10. Dealing with Mass Information

Between 12-15 million people use Skype at any one time. Perhaps double that figure are those connecting through Facebook, Twitter and other social networks. At least two billion people are using an online facility (cf. http://www.peterrussell. com/index2.php), and at any one time an estimated 4 billion people are using a cell phone. This is what we describe as the world of mass information.

More accurately, it is the fruit of a world embroiled in information transactions. Information is the major manufactured good of our time, the phenomenon that engages humans more than anything else. The world revolves around information, in a merry-go-round that becomes faster and more complex by the hour. It is a creative endeavor that billions enjoy, and without which normal life seems well nigh impossible.

Information and complexity

The complexity and subversive nature of this relatively new explosion –the microchip was only released in 1975 –was exemplified vividly in 2011 in the *WikiLeaks* scandal. Launched in 2006 by an Australian Internet activist, Julian Assange. *WikiLeaks* is an international online organization that publishes submissions of private, secret, and classified media from anonymous news sources, news leaks, and whistleblowers. Early releases included documentation of equipment expenditures and holdings in the Afghanistan war, and political corruption in Kenya. In October 2010, the group released a package of almost 400,000 documents called the Iraq War Logs in coordination with major commercial media organizations. In November 2010, *WikiLeaks* collaborated with major global media organizations to release U.S. State department diplomatic cables in redacted format. In April 2011, the group began publishing 779 secret files relating to prisoners detained in the Guantanamo Bay detention camp.

Humans use information to clarify what is going on and to connect meaningfully with the larger concerns of daily existence. Instead of clarification, however, we often encounter baffling complexity, and instead of connection, the plethora of information coming our way can leave us feeling disconnected, confused and at times deprived of all sense of meaning and purpose. Our highly connected mass media web does not simplify reality; rather, it reminds us vividly, and at times, brutally, of the complex world we inhabit.

It is noteworthy however, that while governments condemned *WikiLeaks* for its recklessness and the alleged threat to public security, millions of rank-and-file citizens relished what they perceived to be a courageous action of transparency in a world of sinister secrecy. Millions were both shocked and disgusted at the notion of the United States government spying on the United Nations. The released material, confirmed for the general public the corruption and deception that goes on in the political domain. And although people are not becoming wiser on what to do about it, the fact that such information has entered the public domain gives many people a semblance of being more in touch with the sordid nature of public diplomacy, and offers them at least the prospect of being able to engage more critically with other deviations in the socio-political world.

At a personal level, we all desire to be more aware, informed and better connected. Today's information networks make that possible for us, but usually at a price not immediately obvious. We sacrifice a great deal of personal privacy, a process that frequently makes us vulnerable to exploitation, not merely to computer hackers, but to several social and financial institutions that know more about us than we care to divulge. Unknowingly, we are often lured into cyber anonymity, as people exchange personal, occasionally intimate, information seeking to connect with anonymous others. Cyber addiction is as yet a largely unrecognized form of compulsive voyeurism holding millions of people in its grasp. The mass information culture is changing the very essence of what makes us human.

Information without education

Our educational systems worldwide have not yet adverted to what is really transpiring. We expend time and money teaching basic manual and keyboard skills to youngsters who are already heavily indoctrinated by computer-impact. Exhibiting dexterity of eye and hand, to a degree unknown to previous generations, mere children engage with video games and online stimulation that elevate their psychic potential to thresholds which our formative environment is unable to contain or negotiate constructively. Adding to an already addictive, competitively driven culture, young people –even in poorer nations -are forced into new levels of "functional competence" far in excess of their psychic or developmental growth.

Our educational systems have yet to catch up. We continue to teach subjects in isolation –languages, mathematics, history, and religion – when in fact all of us are being culturally and informationally molded for multi-disciplinary ways of engagement. We waste time and effort teaching basic skills to youngsters already endowed with functional skills far in advance of what we are offering. What we should be imparting is the know-how, the wisdom, to engage the information world with a sense of discrimination and discernment. Even adults are often unable to differentiate between useful and useless information, constructive and destructive outcomes. Frequently, we pursue information without the wisdom to make mature choices.

In Part One, I have already highlighted the addictive lure of modern advertising, whereby millions are seduced into addictive consumerism. Once again, far too many people today lack the critical awareness and accompanying skills to interpret the data, and to make more informed choices. Parents are frequently driven by children's demands; the adult regresses to a kind of adolescent and childlike manipulation. In fact, adult education may now be one of the more urgent needs of our time, towards which we should be directing more of the resources we invest in the education of our youth. (More in O'Murchu 2010).

Evolutionary opportunity

Despite the problematic and negative consequences, which are widely documented, the information revolution marks an evolutionary breakthrough replete with promise and hope. We are witnessing an emergence of unprecedented potential. We have at our fingertips the wisdom and knowledge capable of a radical transformation of our consciousness and our culture. In fact, the transformation is already well underway, but outpacing millions of people who, because of ignorance, are unable (and thus, unwilling) to come on board.

In the 1980s, scientist Peter Russell, proclaimed the coming revolution in his fertile notion of the global brain (Russell, 1982). Russell first recalls the fact that the embryonic human brain passes through two major phases of fetal development. The first is a massive explosion in the number of nerve cells. Starting eight weeks after conception, the number of neurons explodes, increasing by many millions each hour. Five weeks later, this proliferation begins to slow down as early cellular development reaches its critical threshold. At this stage the fetus has most of the nerve cells it will have for the rest of its life.

The brain then proceeds to the second phase of its development, as billions of isolated nerve cells begin making connections with each other, sometimes growing out fibers to connect with cells on the other side of the brain. By the time of birth, a typical nerve cell will communicate directly with several thousand other cells. The growth of the brain after birth consists of the further proliferation of connections. By the time of adulthood many nerve cells are making direct connections with as many as a quarter of a million other cells.

Russell goes on to note a parallel development happening in modern human society. As world population now exceeds seven million people, the number of "cells" in the embryonic global brain is reaching that same critical threshold noted in early fetal development. Billions of human minds are interconnecting into a single integrated network. Reinforced by our global telecommunication capabilities, human society is beginning to look like a planetary nervous system. The global brain is beginning to function with an enhanced creativity, changing the very essence of what it means to be human. Beyond our conventional separate, individual self, today the relational network of our cellular global brain intimately shapes our identity.

Paleontologist and Jesuit priest, Pierre Teilhard de Chardin, first suggested the global brain as an organic process. In 1945, he described a coming "planetization" of humanity, progressively leading to a phase of great socialization; two irreversible and irresistible processes which he predicted would culminate in the emergence of a noosphere, or a global mind. Mind-stuff would become the default position for human, planetary growth and creativity.

In 1993, Gregory Stock proposed a modern vision of super-organism formed by humans and machines, which he calls "Metaman". In this organic metaphor, the analogue of the nervous system is the global brain. The exchanges of information on earth are processing at a high rate and speed, similar to the functioning of a nervous system.

The practical implications are quite momentous and difficult to predict. In many ways the road ahead will depend upon our awareness of what is going on, and the further informed wisdom we need to engage with it in a more enlightened way. The futurist, Ray Kurzweil (2005), spells out some of the daunting challenges that face us. If computing power keeps doubling every eighteen months, as it has done for the last few decades, then sometime in the 2020s there will be computers that can equal the performance of the human brain. From there, it is only a small step to a computer that can surpass our brainpower. There would then be little point in our designing future computers; ultra-intelligent machines would be able to design better ones, and do so at a faster pace.

What happens next is quite unclear, but there are indicators that, in all probability, will be proved to be reasonably accurate. Some propose that humans would become obsolete; machines would become the vanguard of evolution. Others think there would be a merging of human and machine intelligence— downloading our mental abilities into computer-type organisms. The only thing we can confidently predict is that this would be a complete break from the patterns of the past. Evolution would have moved into a radically new realm.

And where would that leave humanity? Precisely where we have been many times when we encountered previous shifts of evolutionary magnitude. Those who are ready may make it through; those who are not ready are likely to lose out – and the number of casualties could exceed millions.

This grim scenario is just too disturbing for most people to consider, and millions simply do not want to know. Yet, there is another way through, a prospect with hope and promise, even if it involves human casualties. It depends on how we take responsibility for the unique giftedness that characterizes us at this evolutionary time: *our capacity for self-reflexive consciousness*. Our ability to rise to this more enlightened response is the evolutionary challenge of this critical and creative historical moment. It is our unique moment of grace, and we need to embrace it with urgency and diligence.

Self-reflexive responsibility

Currently, humans are the creatures most richly endowed with the capacity for self-reflexive consciousness. *We are creation becoming aware of itself.* If evolution is indeed to push on to yet higher levels of integration – particularly towards a new techno-mental synthesis - the most crucial changes will take place in the realm of human consciousness. Our conscious awareness, and the wisdom ensuing therefrom, can catalyze or hinder our ability to flow creatively with evolution's new emergence. In a very real sense, the authentic choices are in our hands – more accurately, in our psyches.

Beyond our preoccupation with making money, and making war, and all the grandiose distractions of the information world itself, we humans are creatures endowed with a unique psychic capacity around which we are called to exercise a novel sense of responsibility at this time. It is a vocational calling with substantial implications, personal and global alike.

In the past we have used the word *vocation* in a narrow religious sense. It often carried otherworld significance, with a disturbing disregard for the surrounding creation, and a dangerously inflated anthropocentrism as if humans were the only God-like creatures endowed with a special vocational status. Today, our human identity is wrapped up in the evolutionary becoming of universal creation itself, and our earthiness provides the formative influences for our growth and development at every level including our spirituality.

Our calling at this time is certainly a *vocation* with an accountability that is both human and divine. What was one time the reserve of an exclusive holiness known as *mysticism*, is now an evolutionary imperative for all of us. It transcends the passive submission often associated with formal religion, and it has little room for a patriarchal God ruling from beyond the sky. Instead the pendulum is swinging towards what indigenous peoples have long known as the *Great Spirit*, the co-creative cosmic life-force, once again reshuffling creation's chaos, and inviting us to daring new horizons which evolution is reshaping at this time.

Like the information explosion, this self-reflexive evolutionary endeavor is complex and to many people it may feel overwhelming. We don't have any choice, other than to follow where the Spirit is leading us. I trust the reflections of this chapter – and of this entire book – will empower us to face the awesome challenges of this critical time. On it depends our entire future.

Handling the transition Wisely

1. Take time to reflect on the visionary statement: "Think globally, act locally."

2. Join a readers group or discussion group, with a focus on important global issues of our time

3. No matter what your age or education is, learn the skills to be able to access online information

4. Develop or improve your ability to think and perceive critically.

5. Aim for wisdom, and be more discriminating on what constitutes useful information.

6. Become acquainted with the notion of *evolution*, and develop skills to talk about it intelligently.

7. Adopt a daily meditation practice – it will help to keep you centered and focused.

8. Learn about the notion of the Great Spirit, as appropriated by indigenous peoples all over our planet.

11. *Economics takes its Toll*

It did not happen immediately after 9/11 – the violent collapse of the twin towers in New York in 2001. It started to unravel about five years later. The US dollar began to lose its value against other international currencies. Within the United States itself, consumerism moved into overdrive, with banks recklessly lending money to insatiable speculators and property tycoons. Meanwhile, millions of dollars were being poured into Iraq and Afghanistan on an annual basis. Life went on as if all was well. It was anything but well, with a deadly cancer eating its way into the US economy – with lethal consequences for every nation on earth.

Finally, in 2008 the Unites States woke up. The major financial institutions were in disarray. Millions were losing their jobs. The cost of living was beginning to soar. Banks had to be bailed out – all because of reckless banking speculators who gambled millions with little or no accountability. Strangely, most of them were granted "immunity", although some did resign. By now the crisis had reached Europe, Japan, India and even China. Something suspiciously fragile seemed to characterize the resilient "unregulated" market. Endless growth came to look more and more like the end of growth.

The institutional death knell

People of deeper vision spoke their truth to power, but as one might expect those in power chose not to listen. The visionaries spoke of the end of Capitalism, or at least the beginning of the end. Who would dare entertain that frightening thought! The impervious divine market might be enduring a crisis – most considered it just a passing blip that could be rectified by more reckless borrowing – the strategy adopted by Gordon Brown in the United Kingdom and by Barak Obama in the United States. No way! Capitalism has to be kept alive even if it is dying on its feet. How right was scripture scholar, Walter Brueggemann (1986, 26), when he wrote:

> A frightened, crushed imagination that has been robbed of power precisely because of fear. Indeed, one can note the abysmal lack of imagination in the formation of policy about either international security or domestic economics. We can think of nothing to do except do more of the same, which generates onlymore problems and more fear.

The financial crisis of the early twenty-first century serves as a useful example of the institutional collapse that is extensive in the modern world but largely unrecognized because of petrified denial. The nation state itself struggles to retain credibility. Even the mighty empire of the United States of America asked for international support in trying to rectify or reverse the financial crisis of 2008. Banking institutions are more vulnerable than anybody had suspected. Education, health care and social systems all show signs of vulnerability, while churches and religions, wrapped up in their own spiritualized imperialism, seem to have little to offer to the confused and frightened masses at this time.

The warnings we did not heed

In 1972, a book entitled *The Limits of Growth* (Meadows & Alia 1972) was published. It was one of the first attempts to use computer programming to trace major trends in three areas: population growth, demand on natural resources, and human consumption. Instead of the limitless growth that was widely assumed at the time, the report indicated that the unregulated market would encounter serious limitations sometime between 2010 and 2050. As one might expect, that Report met with huge resistance and much negative reaction. Thirty years later, when an updated version of the Report was released (Meadows & alia 2004), the precarious predictions could no longer be easily dismissed. A plethora of intervening reports confirmed, time and again, that the pursuit of endless growth is an economic ideology, highly anthropocentric, exhibiting scant regard for the earth and its limited resources.

Our economic ignorance became all the more disturbing. The foundational philosophy based on *scarcity* was shown to be false, yet the adopted economic systems were assumed to flourish on endless resources of abundance. The convoluted theory seems to have been grossly disconnected from any true sense of reality. The leading theories were highly cerebral, and not grounded in the living web of life itself.

Today, despite the cultural economic intransigence that still prevails, more people realize that ours is indeed a universe of abundance, but its potential for flourishing can only be appropriated within the limits of sustainability and mutual encounter. The resources of the earth are not merely commodities that we usurp and purchase for money. The resources are dimensions of a living interactive web in which all features are interrelated and interdependent. Abuse one aspect of the life-chain, and all the others are adversely affected.

Fiscal transparency for all

Although millions are aware of this new insight and information, many people struggle on how to integrate this information into our daily behavior. We have been so indoctrinated in self-perpetuation through accumulation of wealth and the commodification of living systems; we are left largely unaware and unskilled on alternative ways to engage responsibly and creatively. It feels like an enormous burden to take on. Most people don't know where to begin, and many don't want even to think about it.

But as more and more national governments are forced to impose austerity measures, and many poorer nations struggle to survive on depleted resources, the harsh truths are coming home to roost. We have to change our lavish and reckless lifestyles. There seems to be no way out of paying bigger prices for fuel, clothing and even food. Daily we are confronted with the prospect of having to tighten our belts, and learn to live more simply. And most daunting of all, for those more aware of what is happening: *is it too little too late?*

All major institutions are in a state of disarray. What are they about? What purpose do they serve? Have they a future? These are questions that should guide our discernment, but most people are too scared to entertain such fundamental analysis, or worse still are unaware of the need to do so.

Our cultural conditioning also creates serious barriers. The suggested collapse of capitalism can only mean one thing for most people: the revival of *socialism*. We don't seem to have the imaginative versatility to dream of other alternatives. Nor indeed are we capable of discerning what exactly do we mean by socialism in terms of alternatives that have been tried, some successfully, others less so. A great deal of ideological clutter gets in the way, particularly the confusion between Socialism and Marxism, or worse still the identification of Marxism and Communism.

Once again, power raises its ugly head. Socialism, no matter how we define it, involves a sharing of power, where there is less opportunity for the fierce competitor, but more potential for cooperation and mutual enhancement. There is too much to lose for those who like to do business as usual and monopolize for themselves as much as possible; but so much to gain for the millions subdued for too long to the plight of powerlessness and abject poverty.

The shaky financial edifice

Financial disaster is a prospect nobody wants to entertain. In a market economy where money whirls round our world on an electronic roller coaster, it is hard to imagine that there may not be a hole in the wall for the omnipotent visa card we take so much for granted. Even amid the financial crisis that gripped the Eurozone in 2011, for most people business went on as usual. Despite financial pressures, many people tried to sustain a sense of financial normalcy.

It is essential to our psychic and spiritual wellbeing to maintain a stable, economic reliable system. We invest more faith and meaning in money than in any religious truth or dogma. Money is the great God. Yet, God did not come to our rescue in the opening decade of the twenty-first century when bankers in both the United States and Europe drove the economic system into overdrive, creamed off lucrative takings for themselves, sent several banks into liquidation, and could easily have brought the whole system to its knees.

Money is a human invention that can easily be destroyed by human recklessness. Of human origin, and intended for human usufruct, the problem now is that money has been robbed from the people and is almost exclusively controlled by a small gang of speculators serving stringent corporate bureaucracy. Returning money to the people is a challenge awaiting the creative and courageous leaders of the future. It may well become the single biggest challenge facing humanity by the middle of the twenty-first century.

Not many securities left

When money itself becomes problematic, human confidence is shaken to its foundations. Although most people on the planet have limited access to cash, all of us have been indoctrinated to invest money in the accumulation of earthly goods, and the semblance of security that money provides. At a more subtle level, access to wealth means a greater sense of power over life and destiny. In a time of major transition, all our past beliefs will prove unreliable, and progressively will be seen as irrelevant for the alternative future awaiting us.

The financial instability that characterizes the beginning of the twenty-first century is often compared with the great depression of the 1930s. It is a false comparison, another distraction from the crisis confronting us. This time around it is not merely a depression, it is an actual collapse of a foundation we thought was impenetrable. And as we move further into the twenty-first century it is likely to deteriorate, not improve.

Initially, the poor of the earth will once more become the primary victims, and true to form they will exhibit resilience with a sense of ultimate defiance. Emotionally, socially and politically the fall-out will affect the social middle-classes, and to a lesser extent the rich and wealthy. The middle-classes will become increasingly restless, and occasionally violent, as witnessed in the London riots of the Summer of 2011. Many are likely to become disillusioned with politics and politicians, and progressively will lose faith in several major institutions.

For some at least, there will be survival. The price will be a heavy toll for all of us. But it is an evolutionary transition that can be negotiated, and the wisdom to do so will be explored in Part Three.

Handling the Transition Wisely

1. Be aware of what is going on in the socio-economic realm, and rise above denial if at all possible.

2. Be suspicious of politicians and economists who try to blind you with jargon, but are often trying to camouflage their own ignorance.

3. Try and keep a sense of sanity in your work place, especially as more and more people feel financial insecurity.

4. Read about alternative economic systems, and seek out local initiatives exploring other ways of exercising economic accountability.

5. Use your money wisely, invest it ethically, and adopt sustainable life-practices.

6. Remember money is a gift, not primarily a commodity. Whenever possible use it in the service of gifting.

7. Spiritually, aim for the ideal to live simply so that others may simply live.

≈ ◇ ≈

12. *Political Disarray*

The divine right of kings is one of the oldest ideologies known to modern humans. It dates back at least 5,000 years. Even where royal patronage no longer prevails, the privileged status of presidents and prime ministers carries an unmistakable resemblance to kingly imperialism. Kingships dominated the political landscape of the Middle Ages, gradually giving way to another dispensation, namely the nation state. Although never regarded as "divine" (except in cases like the State of Israel), it assumed an exalted status, which theoretically prevails till the present time.

The modern nation state is primarily a European invention that came to the fore after the Peace of Westphalia in 1648. Ironically one of its envisaged functions was to dislodge the monopoly of religion over political activity, while at the same time protecting religious freedom within the context of national governance.

Democratic ambiguity

The State functions and flourishes on the basis of a highly deceptive mystique, described by Richard Falk (2001, 7) as "a profoundly ambiguous political animal."Many nation states are still run as oligarchies. Dictators, using absolute power, relying on the army and police to maintain unquestioned control, operate in several countries. Where the veneer of democracy prevails, people vote for those they wish to govern, often lured by promises that are never fulfilled. Most problematic of all, is the fact that having elected a particular government the people have little or no control over their activity for the subsequent time-span till the next election occurs. Across the so-called democratic world, there is little mutual accountability between people and their elected representatives.

Worse still, most people do not realize the degree to which they have been betrayed by those claiming to uphold democracy. In the year 1994, one hundred twenty three (123) national governments signed a range of international agreements culminating in the establishment of the World Trade Organization (WTO), entrusting widespread powers to transnational corporations, allegedly in the name of liberalizing trade arrangements to the benefit of all. As is now widely known, such agreements, even to this day, favor the rich and powerful and further exploit and deprive the poor. And all these regulations were drawn up largely unknown to the masses who had elected the government negotiators in the first place. The democratically elected consistently betray the trust of the democratic electors.

Ironically, it is the democratically elected, who undermine the nation state itself. Today, it is not individual states that govern, but transnational corporations. They control the wealth, the power, and access to the earth's resources. Corporations exploit national resources, such as the cocoa of Ghana or the vanilla of Madagascar, creating corporate patents whereby it is the corporation that owns the product and not the country where it is primarily produced. This is the bio-piracy that prevails on a widespread scale, and corporations get away with it protected by WTO legislation – agreed in the first place by the representatives of so-called democratic countries.

It is puzzling and disturbing to realize that so few people know what is actually going on. The political landscape is confused and confusing. Indifference and apathy are at the heart of the crisis. Our educational systems collude with the corruption. The people are addicted to power. So addicted that we fail to see the false allurement, and so disempowered that we have come to regard it as normal.

The few that do see through the malaise tend to opt out. They choose not to vote in elections or in referenda because they know what is going on within the dysfunctional system. They choose not to collude with the dysfunctionality, and as we move further into the twenty-first century we can expect more people – particularly the youth – to adopt this stance. It feels like an inferior response –

a cop-out - and is frequently denounced as irresponsible. In fact, it can be the beginning of a consciousness shift without which serious reform of the political system is unlikely to transpire.

The expanding consciousness

Opting out becomes creative when it leads to alternative choices. Thus far only a minority are moving in this direction. The alternative consciousness may not yet be sufficiently coherent to augment this new direction. It begins to happen when those who opt out seek alternative strategies to negotiate their political power. Networking is emerging as a primary articulation of this new direction and will be further explored in Part Three of this book.

Meanwhile, we all inhabit one of those ambiguous spaces that is barren, aimless and destructive. Too many people naively drift along with the prevailing political bureaucracy. It is not easy to confront and challenge the prevailing powers who have themselves well buffered against critique and evaluation. A powerful rhetoric camouflages the corruption and makes the critics feel foolish and disempowered. We are fortunate to live at a time of increased access to the flow of information, to the power of social networking and to other consciousness-raising strategies. Through these, more people are becoming aware, finding their voice in newly empowering ways. The shift in consciousness may seem slow, but there is no doubt that it is happening, and evolution suggests that it will continue to gather momentum.

New scientific insight –reviewed briefly in the last section –is awakening us to a novel and very different understanding of the creation we inhabit and the cosmos to which we belong. As we internalize a deeper sense of creation's own grandeur, we begin to realize that our modes of political and economic engagement are grossly inadequate. Not merely do they fail to engage human creativity, they fare even more inadequately in dealing with the earth and its resources. Not surprisingly, more people realize that our current modes of government are unable to deal appropriately with the major issues facing our world today: global warming, soil erosion, exploitation of natural resources, etc. They look to other agencies to offer more enlightened strategies, and once again networking seems to be an emerging possibility offering more realistic hope for the future.

Towards bioregional re-structuring

Many wars of the twentieth century were fought over the status of nation states. Despite the bloodshed and the unrelenting trail of destruction and suffering, the nation state is still a conflict-ridden entity, with several unresolved issues about land and national boundaries. Nation states are not organic entities; for the most part they are geographical configurations cobbled together to reconcile warring tribes or factions. Both natural and supernatural justifications have been invoked, yet the nation state continues to slide into irrelevance and ineffective performance.

Despite the fact that millions still identify with one or other national identity, this patriotic allegiance is largely a leftover from a previous imperial consciousness. It also reinforces an anthropocentric sense of being in control, which is both deluded and highly destructive for the wider web of life. It is deluded in the sense that finance and markets are largely controlled by transnational corporations and not by nation states. It is highly destructive because it is an alien way for humans to relate with the living earth and the surrounding web of life.

Bioregional configurations would make a great deal more sense. They would link humans with the organicity of the living earth itself, conferring identity and empowerment far in excess of the nation state. The potential in this alternative arrangement will be explored in Part Three.

Handling the Transition Wisely

1. If you feel socially helpless and powerless, explore one step to lift yourself out of your disabling condition.

2. If you find involvement in local government an empowering experience, tell others about it and encourage them to get involved.

3. If you have no involvement in political activity, consider joining a network, where you can share concern around local issues.

4. Take time to read and reflect on what is happening in the larger world.

5. If you follow a particular religion, be vigilant around its exercise of power, and challenge destructive power if at all possible.

6. Adopt a spirituality committed to empowerment in the name of justice, equality and liberation for all who are oppressed or marginalized.

13: *Evolution is Making Us Cosmic*

Of all the transitions engaging humanity at this time, the shifting nature of personal identity is one of the most disturbing, while also remaining one of the most poorly recognized or understood. In the West, and in many parts of Asia, our sense of self tends to be based on nationality, while in Africa it tends to be tribal. An African person is not likely to query one's country of origin, but rather the tribe to which one belongs. In both cases, identity arises from a local affiliation, politically or tribally, with geography determining our sense of being at home in the world, and the parameters in which we feel safe and happy, but also productive and useful.

Educationally, therefore, I develop a sense of self from my family of origin, and over time the circle expands outwards to embrace my local village, town or city. In the African context, and among indigenous peoples, after the family, the tribe is likely to be the next important frame of reference, often depleting the sense of national identity that becomes significant in many other contexts after identifying with village, town or city. National identity is often influenced by religion, generating a quality of patriotism that can easily become narrow and sectarian. Several Muslim states today veer in this direction. Generally, in the modern world, nationality defines the wider sense of affiliation through which we define and understand our place in the world and our responsibilities to the larger web of life.

The Subconscious Shift

What I have described thus far is a conscious process, based on a linear sense of expansion from family through to nation state. At a subconscious level, however, the process is radically different; rapid change is taking place, particularly under the influence of information technology. Scholars such as Robert J Lifton (1999) write about the protean self while Jason Hill (2002) challenges us all to become more consciously cosmopolitan. *Protean* denotes the ability to embrace a multiple rather than a single sense of identity, the ability to honor several loyalties at one time. Negatively, we immediately think of *net surfing* wherein people adopt a range of different personas to suit different purposes. What initially seems like a superficial (and even false) game can, in fact, have strong cultural and personal significance, as highlighted by researchers like Mikela and Philip Tarlow (2002).

The digitalized, fabricated identities that millions adopt in social networking, and affiliations negotiated online, long before a personal encounter, have strange and unexpected parallels with behavior patterns of indigenous peoples. Hence the concept developed by the Barlows of the *digital-aboriginal*. Australian aborigines possess a flexibility of character, and adaptability to varying circumstances, which many "civilized" peoples have lost due to excessive stratification and institutionalized lifestyles. At a more subtle level, how we view the world and engage with it is the crucial issue still awaiting investigation.

This brings me to the insights of the Jamaican-American philosopher, Jason Hill (2002), who claims that our inherited Western tendency to extrapolate a sense of self from our nationality, ethnicity and religion are forms of tribalism that have outlived their usefulness. We need to outgrow these fabricated identities in order to become *cosmopolitan*. For Hill this means becoming trans-national, trans-ethnic, and capable of embracing not one but several religious (spiritual) identities. Hill himself has also grappled with a more fluid sense of psychosexual identity, regarding the dualistic split between heterosexual and homosexual as inadequate for our contemporary cosmopolitan culture.

These are complex insights –of lateral significance - which for the purposes of the present work I can only describe briefly. Important though they are, there is a more foundational issue impacting on our sense of self, and how we engage with the world around us. We are undergoing a massive cultural shift driven by a kind of evolutionary force. Our inherited limited horizons are being stretched almost beyond recognition. A new cosmic consciousness has become our psychic default position and is driving our desires and aspirations in ways we have scarcely begun to recognize. And in the face of this evolutionary breakthrough, our educational systems are failing us on a massive scale.

Our Planetary Universe

Modern science plays a crucial role in the development of this new consciousness. Ever since the evolution of quantum physics throughout the course of the twentieth century, our way of viewing the world, and understanding our place in it, has changed dramatically. According to classical science, which still dominates the academic and industrial worldview as well as our daily practical functioning in the world, cause-and-effect explains all that happens within and around us. And according to the classical view, humans set the pace and dictate the outcomes; humans are in charge.

According to quantum mechanics, there is something bigger, deeper and more complex driving the entire global, cosmic enterprise. The whole is greater than the sum of the parts, and while humans can evoke certain potentialities, they have little or no control over eventual outcomes. *We are carried along by a process of multiple connectedness, engaged intensity and interactions happening faster than the speed of light* (as in the theory of non-locality). It looks like many of the great mystics experienced something of this complex reality, which helps to explain why they are shunned in most rational cultures, while also hinting at the need for a new mysticism in our time.

This new worldview redefines several aspects of our self-understanding, while also providing a challenge to engage differently with every aspect of the created universe. We are invited to expand our sense of organicity, viewing the entire creation as essentially alive, with a dynamism that determines the life-quality of every other creature, ourselves included. In this scenario, we are not a superior life form. Aliveness belongs first and foremost to the universe, mediated to us through the Earth, with its range of chemical and physiological process that makes human life possible.

Life, therefore, is not merely a biological outcome, embodied primarily in human beings. Life is a process, and humans are events rather than objects. Everything in creation grows, changes and develops. Life is more about becoming rather than about being.

And the neat demarcation lines that have served us in the past are no longer seen as central. In fact they may be totally false. I refer particularly to our felt need for beginnings and endings. Cosmologists are moving strongly to the view that we live in *a multi-verse* without beginning or end. Infinity is our destiny.

All life is a continuum, moving through transformational transitions. Death is a rite-of-passage, an ending that marks a new beginning.

These insights readily indicate the foundational interconnectedness of all things. Nothing makes sense in isolation. For humans this is a formidable challenge so strongly indoctrinated into being the superior species with the mandate to conquer and control the dead inert matter of a physical universe. For so long, we have objectified and commodified the creation to which we intimately belong, and without which our lives have neither purpose nor meaning. We face a process of change and conversion far more demanding than religious belief ever required.

Our cosmic belonging

Several transitions now require our attention and discernment. Our superior sense of domination and control, whereby we considered ourselves closer to God and to ultimate meaning, is a misguided arrogance we need to leave behind. Our uniqueness is not in our isolation or in our superior status, but in the identity that begins to emerge from our sense of belonging and the inter-relatedness that arises from that cosmic affiliation.

What sounds very new in our present situation, is in fact something we have known for most of our time on this earth. We took our identity from the cosmic web of life, and instinctively understood ourselves as servants to an evolving cosmic story. It is only in recent millennia, less than 8,000 years ago, that we adopted the patriarchal, self-inflated role of manipulating the surrounding creation and reducing it as an object for human usufruct. Now we realize the trail of destruction we have left in our wake, and the need for radical readjustment, if we wish to continue to live meaningfully as citizens whose essential identity is defined by our belonging and not by our self-centered arrogance.

As often happens in the big story of evolution, the impetus for this new awareness is not coming from those we look to for wisdom and guidance, whether educationally, politically or spiritually. The new cosmic awareness is emerging from a diverse range of ground-up movements, many of which seem esoteric, anarchic and too counter-cultural to be embraced with comfort. As indicated in Part Two, it is not those well versed in rational argument who pave the way to a better future, but frequently those lateral thinkers inspired by a new mysticism, deeply rooted in the living earth itself. That earthy grounding, so essential for negotiating all the transitions of this time, is the topic of our next Section.

Handling the Transition Wisely

1. If you have not already explored a sense of being a cosmic creature and a planetary citizen, take one step to embrace that new awareness.

2. Take time to inform yourself of emerging insights from science and cosmology - on our changing understanding of the world today.

3. Remember the adage – and act on it: "Think globally; act locally."

4. Time and money permitting, explore a new country and its culture.

5. Adopt a daily meditation practice, which will expand your consciousness in a more cosmic direction.

6. Immerse yourself more in the natural world, love the soil, and cultivate earth-produce if at all possible.

$$\approx \Diamond \approx$$

14. *We Are the Earth: Like it or not!*

Global warming signifies a great deal more than an environmental predicament of our time. It is a symptom of a progressive breakdown exacerbated largely by human beings. Planet Earth has known many catastrophes –e.g., major extinctions – over its lifespan of four billion years. Paradoxically, the earth needs internal turbulence, destruction and disarray to continue its creative growth and development. Global warming may well be one of those paradoxical disruptions. However, among scientists there is widespread consensus that humans are adding to the destructive impact. And it's all down to a fundamental ignorance, resulting in a dysfunctional relationship with the web of life itself.

Formal religions have contributed significantly to this problem. Christianity has long emphasized that humans are not meant to be too attached to the material world, and to the organic web of life. Frequently, it is portrayed as a vale of tears, the realm of sin and temptation, a human abode in which we are not meant to feel at home, a base from which we are meant to escape to true happiness and fulfillment in another world. Elements of this otherworld escapist spirituality can be detected in most of the major religions known to humanity today.

The earth body

The ignorance I allude to above initially arose from religion, and has been absorbed by politics and market forces in more recent times. For long, religion has objectified the earth, viewing it as an artifact that exists for human use and benefit. It is soul-less materiality deemed to be inferior to soulful people. It is a passive, inert substance to be influenced by intelligent humans.

Despite advances in earth sciences in recent decades – geology, geophysics, oceanography, and biology – humans still exhibit an extensive ignorance about the living earth and its organic dynamics. The embodied nature of planet earth is still a relatively new idea to millions of humans. As a corporeal entity, it exhibits all the organic processes upon which the human body thrives. These insights are much better understood in our time thanks to the pioneering work of James Lovelock (1979; 1988) and others on what is now known as the *Gaia Theory*.

Initially formulated in the 1970s, the Gaia Theory posits that the organic and inorganic aspects of planet Earth have evolved together as a single living, self-regulating system. Equipped with an inner wisdom –akin to the immune system of the human body, the earth-body automatically controls elements like global temperature, atmospheric content, ocean salinity, and other factors, to the benefit of its growth and development. For instance, even though the luminosity of the sun –the Earth's heat source –has increased by about 30 percent since life began almost four billion years ago, the living system has reacted as a whole to maintain temperatures at levels suitable for life.

Because the earth-body is so endowed, then all corporeal organisms carry the same life-enhancing properties and potentialities. And without this foundational empowerment, not even human beings could survive or flourish on earth. We are the earth in every dimension of our truest selves.

The Earthiness of the Human body

For healthy functioning, the human body relies not merely on the earth, but on the entire universe, a notion captivated elegantly by Judy Cannato (2006, 65) when she writes:

> The water in your body contains primordial hydrogen formed in the first seconds of the Big Bang. The carbon atoms that formed you came together after the explosion of a supernova. The concentration of salt in your body matches the concentration of salt in the ancient seas. Your cells are direct descendants of unicellular organisms that developed billions of years ago. You see because chlorophyll molecules mutated,

so that like plant leaves, your eyes can capture the light from the sun. And in your mother's womb your tiny body repeated the whole process of multi-cellular life on earth, beginning with a single cell, and then developing greater and greater complexity.

This cosmic process impacts upon human growth and development through our earthiness. The earth provides the grounding through which the creative dynamics of the universe animate and energize the human body. Human reproduction is not merely a biological process between a male and a female; it encapsulates complex field influences of cosmic proportion, but mediated and facilitated through our earthiness. It is the creativity of the living earth that brings into being all new forms of life.

The book of Genesis captivates something of this earthy organicity in the very naming of the first human, Adam, which in Hebrew means "of the earth." And the earliest uses of the name in Genesis is not to denote a significant male, but to both the male and female of the earth-species. In Genesis 1:27 "Adam" is used in the collective sense, denoting all humankind. And in Gen.5:2, we read "Male and female God created them; and blessed them, and called their name Adam..."

Resonant with our Earthy Identity

For well over 90% of our time on earth, humans lived close to the earth, and interacted with the earth body in a convivial, interdependent mode. The flow of daily life, from sunrise till sunset, and the rhythm of seasonal changes were reflected in the lifestyle and values which humans adopted. We ate foods that belong uniquely to the seasons, having extracted them directly from the living earth itself. We used potions and medicines congruent with the earth's own healing potential. Cloths were woven from the ingredients of the local environment. Consciously, or otherwise, we befriended local bioregions in their natural growth and development. Humanity and Earth were intimately interconnected.

Indigenous peoples of our time vaguely reflect this interactive organicity. While still echoing an inherited sense of this ancient sacredness, even tribal, first-nation peoples exhibit a modern consciousness that undermines in practice what they hold in theory. They speak freely and elegantly of the sacredness of the earth, yet they often adopt highly patriarchal social structures, and in not a few cases, are being decimated by diseases and addictions characteristic of the "advanced" culture of Western society.

The disconnection can be traced back some 8,000 years to the shadow side of the Agricultural Revolution, when a new rational philosophy denounced humans for being too enmeshed in the surrounding creation and encouraged them to differentiate into the separate, autonomous creatures they were meant to be under the rule of a patriarchal sky God. In historical and cultural terms, we can now understand that move to have been a type cultural stillbirth in which humans were brutally separated from the sustaining womb of the earth itself. Even to this day it has left us with a numbed sense of painful disconnection, perhaps something like a child that has never known its real mother. In our estrangement we search for a fulfillment that always seems to elude us, and all too easily we succumb to the naive religious belief that it will all be rectified in a life hereafter.

The problem is not with what will happen hereafter, but with the here and now. We are not at home where the creative God (what the indigenous peoples call the Great Spirit) has birthed us, with all the resources at our disposal to grow and flourish, to evolve and become whole. Earth is our true home – in both evolutionary and spiritual terms. Paradoxically, more and more people are beginning to realize this. Human intuition and imagination is reawakening a wisdom deep within. What to do with that wisdom is where the problem often becomes acute.

Some take their concern to their church or religious source, only to be met with a bland stare, or worse still, stern words of denunciation. Fortunately, others discern more reflectively and seek out spiritual accompaniment of a more mystical foundation, and this is a much more promising route in which to reclaim our primordial affiliation with the earth body. At this juncture we are entering the new spiritual landscape explored in the next Section of this book.

Back to the earth

Meanwhile, we face another formidable transition. Today, an estimated 80% of human beings live in cities, with several sprawling suburbia that have little or no connection with the natural environment. Such conditions are inimical to soulful living. Within a few kilometers of such degradation, other forms of earth-depletion take place: logging of woodland, stripping of topsoil, excessive exploitation of mineral resources. It happens in Brazil, in the Philippines and in several African nations. Humans are starved for earth intimacy, while the earth itself is being brutalized for human wealth and gain.

And we wonder why people are so unhappy, and why human alienation is so widespread at this time! How could any species, so disconnected from its nourishing womb, know happiness of fulfillment? Our earthiness is not some material object apart from, or over against, our true selves. It is inherently and intimately part and parcel of who we are and what we are. It is central to our God-given identity and the entire meaning of our existence. Re-appropriating our reconnection with the living earth will remain one of the single greatest challenges for humanity as we move deeper into the twenty-first century.

Handling the transition wisely

1. Cultivate a garden, or garden-plot, if at all possible.

2. Use organic food whenever possible.

3. Make yourself familiar with the process of photosynthesis, the nourishing foundation of all organic life.

4. Participate in organizations seeking justice for the earth, e.g., Friends of the Earth.

5. Engage in rituals that celebrate the seasons and earth's life-giving potential.

6. Recycle waste conscientiously.

7. Cultivate a spirituality that loves creation rather than demonizes it.

15. *After Religion, Spirituality Endures*

Spirituality became a buzzword throughout the closing decades of the twentieth century. Different commentators offer various definitions, but all have one thing in common: a *desire or aspiration to move beyond formal religion*. Spirituality is another one of those transitional concepts. It denotes not so much a rejection of the past (in this case, of religion) as rather an assertion that the past is no longer relevant, useful or meaningful. Something new is unfolding, and nebulous and vague though it may be; spirituality captivates something of its deeper meaning.

Is spirituality an attempt to return religion to its primary purpose? Probably, yes! But that begs the question that may be central to the reflections on this subject: what is the primary purpose of religion? Advocates of formal religion are quite clear about its function: a) to provide a creedal statement to which all followers are asked to assent; b) to develop an ethical code for upright human living; c) to evolve a structure for worship, upon which all followers can agree. All religions broadly agree with those elements, while interpreting and implementing them in vastly different ways.

Spirituality

As employed in modern usage these are some of the key elements employed in the notion of Spirituality:

-It is an articulation of the human search for meaning in life, a pursuit shared by humans of every time and culture.

-It predates formal religion by several thousand years.

-It comes from deep within (often interpreted as individualistic), uniquely personal and veering more in the direction of meditation, inner experience, and mysticism.

-Its worth and value are often judged by good feelings; how to interpret personal experience is crucial to how we evaluate the meaning of spirituality in people's lives.

-It is sometimes identified with esoteric practices such as tarot readings, invoking spirit-beings, drug-induced ecstasy, soul-migration, and connection with the dead (ancestors).

-It is widely connected with a love for nature and a desire to live in more convivial and responsible ways with the natural environment.

-Morally, it veers in the direction of situation ethics; if it feels good it must be right. External ethical codes are often considered suspect.

-It tends to view external authority in a negative light, particularly, that which emanates from patriarchal/ hierarchical systems.

-Faith in a divine source is common, but frequently perceived to be transpersonal (often interpreted by outsiders as impersonal), and more readily perceived in nature, or in inner solitude, rather in the transcendent realm adopted by formal religions.

-The need for ritual is often explored, adopting models from indigenous peoples, with an emphasis on natural/seasonal cycles.

-Women, rather than men, explore spirituality.

-Heavy emphasis on the interconnectedness of all things; a strong dislike for dualistic divisions, and an intuitive sense that the Divine belongs to a relational mode, rather than being perceived as an isolated authoritarian figure in some distant heaven.

The challenge

As a transitional phenomenon, spirituality offers some significant namings of what has outlived its relevance in our time, and what needs to be reclaimed to empower us for the evolving future. In some ways, the reclaiming is characterized by great age and deep wisdom, radically different from the perception and denunciation of New Age weirdness.

These are some of the transformative elements:

Divine Mystery: Unknowingly, for the greater part, spirituality seeks to liberate God from the hidebound doctrines and rituals of formal religion, and from the reductionistic anthropocentrism in which we try to mold God in our image and likeness. One detects a reawakening of the God who is present in the whole of creation and in every living being, a pervasive sacredness that indigenous people – past and present – name as the Great Spirit (explored at length in O'Murchu 2012). And there certainly is ambiguity on the personal nature of this divine life force, a challenge that needs to be assessed positively rather than negatively. In seeking to transcend the reductionistic anthropocentrism, we are not denying the personal dimension of Holy Mystery, but rather reframing it in a larger, cosmic context.

Divine capacity for relating: The strong emphasis on connectedness and relatedness is actually a reassertion of one of the oldest and most pervasive insights shared by all religions, especially through their mystical expressions: namely belief in a Trinitarian God. Every religion has a doctrine of the Trinity, sometimes dispatched to the mystical wing as in the Sufism of Islam, or the Cabbala of Judaism. The Christian version is well known for its numerical puzzle of trying to fit three into one, or for the doctrinal controversies of early Christian centuries, with both features distracting heavily from the underlying archetypal truth: God is primarily about an intense capacity for relating. In this context, spirituality is pioneering a significant retrieval of a deep, ancient truth.

Outgrowing dualisms: The distinction between the sacred and the secular, between this world and the next, between spirit and matter, are humanly contrived splits that seriously deviate from the presence of the sacred in all things, including the great paradox of creation-and-destruction. This dualistic splitting is pervasive in the new Catholic missal introduced in 2011. Once, again spirituality is providing a long-overdue corrective.

The Internal focus: The strong pursuit of inner personal fulfillment –often interpreted as excessive individualism – is an element that requires considerable discerning attention. To what extent is this leaning a reaction – and a compensation – for a previous religious indoctrination that left many people feeling empty and betrayed within themselves? Was the emphasis so much on external observation and legal obligation that millions were left starved for inner meaning, now being unashamedly pursued in the spiritual awakening of our time?

By what authority? Similarly, we question the nature and purpose of religious authority. In the inherited religions, God is portrayed as the supreme ruler, governing from a distant heaven, validating those on earth deemed to be worthy of representing this patriarchal figurehead, predominantly males. This divinely mandated hierarchical control has lost credibility on a massive scale in recent decades and all indications are that it will continue to do so. In this regard, spirituality is simply reinforcing a cultural paradigm shift that is already well advanced in its evolutionary trajectory.

Towards a new integration: All the great religions claim to be pursuing an essential oneness that characterizes the totality of living reality, but the dualistic splitting makes it impossible to realize this core sense of unity. Spirituality moves much more radically in this direction, seeking to reconnect with the sacred throughout the whole creation, and not merely in a distant heaven. Spirituality also supports the care of the body (earthy and personal) and not merely the soul. While spirituality seeks to integrate all life-experiences, religion tends to split and divide.

Relationality to the fore

It is the relational connection however that probably provides the central breakthrough, and the single greatest challenge in handling this transition creatively. America feminist scholar, Charlene Spretnak (1992) provides this definition: *Spirituality is the aspect of human existence that explores the subtle forces of energy in and around us and reveals to us profound interconnectedness*. The deeper the exploration goes, the more we encounter a fresh transparency where connectedness and not fragmentation characterizes the world of our experience. In a world so serrated by exploitation, pain and suffering, this is indeed a bold claim, on that defies credulity.

The secret to unraveling the profound wisdom of this definition rests on the notion of energy, which will be explored at length in Part Three. We are entering the weird and mystical world of quantum physics. Energy is the life-stuff of which everything is constituted and on which everything flourishes. Energy exists in abundance, in fact, in extravagance. And energy thrives through inter-relationality.

Just as many scientists find the notion of energy thriving through inter-relationality a hard concept to understand, so too do religionists. Spirituality and quantum physics share an amazing common thread, as baffling as it is profound. Both embrace and endorse the foundational role of relationship, as the core dynamic from which everything obtains meaning, and without which meaning cannot flourish. This partnership of science and spirituality may be one of the most exciting and empowering cultural breakthroughs of the twenty-first century.

Handling the Transition Wisely:

1. Be wary of religious dogmatism; it can undermine the creative spirit.

2. Be open to the mystery that surrounds us in the natural world.

3. Cultivate an interest in the great religions, and in spiritual movements that help to broaden our understanding of the mystery of life.

4. Adopt a daily meditation practice, and follow it as faithfully as possible.

5. Read and reflect on the new spiritual awakening of this time.

6. Invest your money according to ethical principles, and not merely for the best interest rates.

7. Participate in new religious rituals, and broad en your horizons of spiritual engagement.

≈ ◇ ≈

16. *Cooperation in Defiance of the Future*

Is it possible that human beings are not inherently evil or intrinsically self-interested and materialistic, but are of a very different nature –an empathic one –and that all of the other drives we have considered to be primary –aggression, violence, selfish behavior, acquisit6iveness – are in fact secondary drives that flow from repression or denial of our most basic instinct?

Jeremy Rifkin

From a very young age, we indoctrinate our children to be fierce competitors. The drive is subconscious for the greater part. An internal script informs us that they are born into a brutal world and will have to be brutal themselves if they stand any chance of surviving. So, we ensure they get all the up-to-date gadgetry which advertising imposes, all the goodies their peers exhibit. They will be dressed according to the prevailing fashions and do the stereotypical behaviors expected in the culture. They must perform well at school, and above all excel in examination results.

The survival of the fittest is not merely a well-worn neo-Darwinian cliché, it is an internal instinct that drives most of our human behavior. That is the way we are, it is the essential nature of the human animal. For over twenty years now, researchers such as Jane Goodall, Frans de Waal, and others have been alerting us to an assumption we have naively taken for granted, namely that we have inherited from our animal and primate ancestors the tendency to be competitive even to the point of being violent towards our own kind. This is not the evidence encountered by those who observe animals and primates in their natural conditions of the wild.

The cooperative animal.

Most of our major conclusions about animal behavior are based on observations of those caged for laboratory experimentation. One does not need to be an academic researcher to see the fallacy of this procedure. Lock a pet in a cage for even a short period of time and it will become agitated, aggressive and violent. Not so, with many of those same creatures when observed in their natural environment. And interestingly, many animals (and primates) first become defensive and violent when their habitat is disturbed, or they perceive a threat that such an intrusion is imminent.

Most animals live in a convivial and cooperative fashion. Competitive behavior, which sometimes can be violent, as in grooming or mating, serves other interactions within the larger group nearly always resulting in more elaborate forms of cooperation, to procure the welfare of the overall group. On the big scale, cooperation is far more widespread than competition.

A self-fulfilling prophecy is also at work here. Academic research is so convinced of the violent nature of life, including human behavior, that outcomes, which fail to verify this observation, are held to be suspect. In such research we see what we want to see, and rationalize our way out of that which does not fit our paradigm of understanding. This is particularly the case in primatology, the study of our primate ancestors. Chimpanzees have been studied in great detail, and their often-violent behavior has been noted time and again. Scant attention has been given to the *bonobos*, a subgroup of the chimps, who are renowned for their cooperative, altruistic behavior, with a strong matriarchal structure, and an extensive use of sexual intimacy to resolve disagreement and conflict. Why not use that group as model and inspiration for how humans could be? Presumably, because it does not suit the dominant patriarchal culture and all the cultural presuppositions that have been sanctioned over time.

The cooperative human

In the opening decade of the twenty-first century, a new consciousness around human cooperation began to unfold, culminating in the publication of some highly significant texts. These include Sarah Blaffer Hrdy, *Mothers and Others*, Jeremy

Rifkin's *The Empathic Civilization*, and Dacher Keltner's *The Compassionate Instinct*. All these works depict a very different understanding of what it means to be human. We are programmed not for competition but for cooperation. Altruistic behavior is our default position. We are innately attuned to be compassionate, caring and cooperative. In seeking the wellbeing and good of others, we realize our highest potential.

Once more we find ourselves in the web of a shifting awareness. The dominant culture still clings fiercely to competitive instinct and generously rewards those that play the game –and win! And such is the glamor surrounding the winning; it is relatively easy to subdue the loser to oblivion. In a world where many are perpetually condemned to be losers, the culture will be quick to conjure up compensations; it becomes all too obvious why hedonistic behavior features so strongly across the planet.

It is the dominant culture itself that creates the abuse of drugs, gambling and excessive hedonism. Even the compulsive urge of having to be a winner all the time takes its toll on those who seem to be successful in life. Not surprising, therefore, we discover, every now and again, that a particular drug cartel is owned and run by a highly successful businessman, of allegedly high moral repute! The cult of fierce competition corrodes the integrity of even the most resilient. In truth, there are no winners in a system that allows no space for vulnerability and failure.

Shifting the focus from competition to cooperation will not be easy. We will be working against the grain and will encounter massive opposition. And yet we have to honor what is deep in our hearts and what is beginning to be seen - culturally and humanly - a more responsible thing to do. In evolutionary terms we are also faced with a daunting choice, because, it seems, that evolution favors the cooperation that leads to more intimate relating, and not the neo-Darwinian victor in the survival of the fittest.

Towards a more collaborative culture

Throughout the course of the twentieth century the Trade Union movement featured in most industrial workplaces. Workers rights became an integral feature of a work place, striving to be more equitable and empowering. As unions gained cultural significance, they also adopted the power dynamics of the industrial system they sought to alter. And the culture of the work place also began to change under the progressive nature of the mechanization of work. Thus the unions lost much of their potential as a force for empowering change.

In most spheres of life, from major bureaucratic institutions to the home and family system, we note throughout the twentieth century a gradual liberalization from patriarchal power, and a trend towards more democratic participation. The fundamental cooperative strain, noted above, seemed to be reasserting itself. And as it did so, people wanted more. However, as more was granted we also evidenced the disempowering co-dependency whereby people were unable to assume the new responsibilities they had been demanding. In psychic and cultural terms, they were locked into a co-dependent trap, freedom from which would demand not merely an alteration in behavior, but more significantly a change in inner disposition. That struggle for a new integration characterizes our time, and is unlikely to be resolved in the foreseeable future.

There has been a shift in power, but we are still a long way from an empowering culture that will prize cooperation over competition. Patriarchal institutions are still in place quite similar to what prevailed a hundred years ago. We have Presidents, CEOs, Bankers and Religious leaders who still exercise control from the top down. Things have shifted in the sense that those at the top delegate through several layers of bureaucracy, but most of the bureaucrats belong to the power-caste, and the rank-and-file do not trust them. They perceive them to be clones of those who seek absolute control.

In our modern bureaucracies, and in the religious sphere as well, there are no effective structures for real involvement of the rank-and-file. Intuitively millions know this, but don't know what to do about it. This is the great source of human alienation. In the face of it, all the attempts on earth at empowerment from the top down will not persuade or convince the masses. The collective consciousness seeks an alternative form of empowerment, a more participative and egalitarian form that engages the real issues of daily life.

The model that does offer some promise –already named in earlier sections –is that of networking. It is likely to become a much more persuasive option as we move into the twenty-first century, carrying hope for empowerment not merely for humans, but for the suffering earth itself as well. I will explore its potential in Part Three.

Handling the Transition Wisely

1. Whether at work, in school, or in the neighborhood, encourage people to opt for win-win outcomes rather than win-lose strategies.

2. Get involved in neighborhood projects that foster cooperation along with the enhancement of local community development.

3. In the workplace, encourage collaborative endeavor rather than unilateral power.

4. Make yourself more familiar with systems theory and group dynamics thus empowering you to challenge and unmask unhealthy forms of power.

5. Work for peace and reconciliation – in your own heart, and with people from whom you have become estranged.

6. Be wary of any behaviors that encourage children to be overly competitive.

7. Support the vision and work of the United Nations in any way you can.

8. In the religious domain move away from language lauding God as all-powerful.

17. *Christian Salvation in an Earthly Paradise*

Paradise in this world cannot be honored unless those with power and privilege release their grip on benevolent paternalism.

Rita N. Brock & Rebecca Parker.

The shift in spirituality explored in the previous sections impacts strongly on our understanding of human destiny. According to the inherited view, humans were born into the world to continue God's work, to struggle against the forces of evil, in an imperfect and sinful world, and having done their best –and with God's grace – would hopefully escape from this vale of tears to enjoy eternal happiness in a life hereafter.

The process of *salvation* (known as *redemption* in Christian faith) followed a kind of linear progression, from God, through the problematic creation, and proceeding on to heavenly salvation, or eternal damnation. In the Great Eastern religions the process is understood to be more cyclic than linear; the person may have to be reincarnated several times before eventually escaping into the fullness of divine life (Nirvana).

A problematic anthropology

Three features of this paradigm are noteworthy. God is portrayed as a kind of capricious manager of a highly problematic natural order, with the human acting as a kind of ambassador but hopelessly inadequate for the task. All three participants: *God*, the *human*, and *the creation* seem skewed from the start. It is assumed that God knows what God is about, and the fewer questions we ask, the better. God is in charge, and we humans are not meant to understand the mysterious workings of God. For spiritual people of our time, that sounds like explaining things away, rather than attempting a meaningful explanation. The desire for more coherent meaning is a central feature of the new paradigm emerging at this time.

Next, is the human! Original Sin is the crucial factor here based on a preposterous myth that modern peoples consider not merely incredible but ludicrous. A battle between good and bad angels is supposed to have taken place in Heaven; the good won and the bad lost. The bad ones were kicked out of Heaven (by God?) and landed on earth. They began to propagate, and thus all human life thereafter is tainted by the rebellious nature of the original progenitors. For all time to come, humans will carry this fundamental flaw. Rescue (i.e., salvation) can only happen through a special favor from God, known as grace, and that is made possible by the Death and Resurrection of the Christian Jesus. And only Jesus can make it possible for people of every race, culture and religion. Only through the power of the Cross can humans be saved.

Salvation here means escape –from this vale of tears, the sinful problematic world, which was never intended for humans in the first place. By a kind of heavenly freak-event we ended up here. And this place, planet Earth, can never be our home in any meaningful sense.

The anthropology is pathetic, and the cosmology is worse. According to the Original Sin theory, humans are the pinnacle of creation, and if they are flawed (which they are), consequently everything else in creation must also be corrupt and corruptible. Creation seems to be a kind of temporary abode for humans to work out their salvation before the creation itself goes through a cataclysmic end, the famous end of the world scenario, in which God will gather all the nations (peoples) for a grand final judgment of all peoples. The created world – cosmos and all the planets - will be destroyed forever. Paradise will take over in a world beyond, where those who are saved and redeemed will live with God forever.

Paradise Revived

Millions still believe this primitive, preposterous myth, and it flourishes in several fundamentalist religions, Christian and others. It offers a semblance of hope for the millions condemned to poverty, anomie, exploitation and cruel suffering. It certainly brings consolation, but little by way of liberation. It promises salvation in a life hereafter but does little to improve or transform life here on earth. Nor has it much to offer the suffering earth itself at this time of so much exploitation of natural resources and the devastation of the web of life itself. In other words, it is a paradigm that offers no long-term hope either for humanity or for the home planet.

In the closing decades of the twentieth century, theologians began to acknowledge the spurious myth that feeds and sustains our theories of redemption. They offered alternative views to the myth of violent redemption, and suggested new insights into the Christian story of the death and Resurrection of Jesus. However few went as far as the collaborative endeavor of two feminist scholars Rita N. Brock and Rebecca Parker whose intensive research (Brock & Parker 2008) provides a framework for reform conducive to the paradigm shift being outlined in this book.

Their major study is entitled: *Saving Paradise*, with the following subtitle: "How Christianity traded love of this world for Crucifixion and Empire." Having studied early iconography of the Christian crucifix, they noted that our popularly used version of the Christian Cross depicts a tortured, emaciated Jesus, wearing a crown of thorns and spattered in blood. This is the most widely used version of the crucifix, one that probably portrays quite accurately what crucifixion was like, but surprisingly not used extensively by Christians until the tenth century of the Christian era. The oldest known replica of this kind of crucifix, which is visible to this day, is that of the Gero Cross in the Cathedral of St. Peter and Maria in Cologne, Germany. Its date is that of 965 CE.

Prior to the tenth century it seems that Christians for their devotion and worship used a form of the Cross displaying a glorious risen Jesus, rather than a tortured emaciated image, or occasionally a cross with no human figure on it. What brought about the change?

Brock and Parker propose two major developments:

a) The launch of the first Crusade in 1095 in which Pope Urban II instructed the crusaders to wear over their outer garments the image of a tortured crucified Jesus, presumably to justify their torture of the infidels, and to validate the sacrifice of their own lives in defence of the faith.

b) St. Anselm's Atonement theory that was published in his major written work, *Cur Deus Homo*, in 1098.

Both of these developments declared categorically that entry into paradise, i.e., life in a world hereafter, outside and above this material creation, was the goal of Christian life; it could only be achieved by suffering in solidarity with the cruel sufferings of Jesus on the Cross. In other words, the more we suffered the greater our chances of attaining that quality of holiness that would be rewarded with admission into paradise in a life to come.

Today, as already indicated, the theory of violent redemption is the subject of sustained theological critique. Indeed it means little to reflective Christians generally. However, there is a more subtle deviation which Brock and Parker highlight, which is the central insight of their inspiring work. The word *paradise* had a totally different meaning in the first Christian millennium than in the second. Equating paradise with life hereafter is almost entirely a development that happens from the tenth century onwards. Prior to that time the word denoted something entirely different.

Paradise in the first Christian millennium denoted *the inherent sacredness of creation* itself, and in this context, salvation meant working to bring about the transformation of creation so that it would more vividly manifest the divine sacredness. Paradise in this context is almost the complete opposite of our conventional understanding, which only began to transpire after the tenth century.

In their scholarly research, Brock and Parker examined closely the frescoes of the Roman catacombs, noting, as other researchers have done, that there are no images of God sitting in judgment, no crucifixes, and no depictions of a crucified Jesus – as one would expect in this forum so unique in the history of martyrdom. Instead, the prevailing imagery is that of garden scenes, lush natural growth, trees, shrubs and a flourishing creation. Denoting what? Namely, that these early martyrs seem to have embraced their intense sufferings, not to escape to a paradise beyond this world, but as the price they were paying to help to bring about justice here and now, and thus enhance the beauty and goodness of God's creation.

Cosmic Salvation

Saving Paradise is one of several written works of recent decades marking a significant shift in our understanding of our relationship with God and with God's divinity at the heart of creation. These new insights profoundly alter our anthropology, our understanding of the human in the midst of God's creation.

Science illuminates, and in fact deepens, this process. Today, we know there is no place or reality outside and beyond our universe. Ours is an open-ended creation in which the human categories of inside and outside carry no meaning. There is no outside –only an enduring within-ness. In this scenario, our human task –our salvation –is to work towards a greater awakening of the true nature of universal reality, to bring to greater consciousness and clarity the paradise that is creation itself. This paradise is on its way towards fuller realization, an evolutionary advancement that will benefit creation itself and illuminate more clearly the divine creativity forever animating and nourishing the evolving process.

As humans we bring a distinctive contribution to the process. Endowed uniquely as we are with the capacity for self-reflexive consciousness, we carry a privileged responsibility for making transparent the consciousness (energy) that sustains the cosmic creative process. Instead of seeing ourselves as puny helpless creatures, waiting on a capricious deity to save us through the torture of his beloved child, we are cosmic planetary beings entrusted with an onerous evolutionary responsibility, namely to give our lives in co-creating right-living (justice) that will augment the flourishing of creation as intended by the divine creator.

I suspect many of the major problems confronting humanity today arise precisely because we don't know who we are, and our way of operating in the world is based on an appalling ignorance. We are dysfunctional creatures, still influenced by a dysfunctional anthropology, which is largely arising from a primitive punitive spirituality. It is an anthropology that persistently alienates us from the creation to which we belong intimately and integrally.

Nelson Mandela echoed a similar refrain in his remark that it is not our weaknesses that characterize us but our greatness (Mandela, 1994, Inaugural Speech). If we adopted and pursued that insight, what a different world we could co-create together! What hope we would generate – for each other, and for the suffering earth as well!

Handling the Transition Wisely

1. Strive to appropriate in your daily life a more earth-centered spirituality.

2. Join or support an organization committed to the work of justice in our world.

3. In Christian language, shift the emphasis from salvation via death (mortality) to salvation via life (natality).

4. Promote a Christian understanding that Jesus suffered to rid the world of meaningless suffering, and never exonerated suffering for its own sake.

5. Explore alternative rituals to mark the annual liturgy of the Death and Resurrection of Jesus.

18. *Making Sense of Relationships in a culture of fluidity*

In former times, if people wanted to explore the deeper mysteries of life, they would often enter the seclusion of a monastery or hermitage. For many of us today, however, intimate relationships have become the new wilderness that brings us face to face with all our gods and demons.

John Welwood.

Despite the cultural turmoil around relationships and intimacy in modern life, most people still exhibit widely shared aspirations. We imagine that we should be able to establish a rich and satisfying relationship with someone we love. And despite the widespread publicity around marital instability and family breakdown, most people desire a life-long relationship, and the option for family life still commands extensive support across all cultures.

Despite these noble aspirations, the landscape of modern love and intimacy exhibits much strain, ambiguity and fragmentation.

For millions of people, true love is an illusive ideal. Expectations vary enormously; emotional involvement tends to be both fragile and intense; conflict evokes fears around insecurity and lack of fidelity; media portrayals of betrayal and experimentation impact quite deeply on perceptions and expectations; for many couples, trust is always on trial. On top of all that, human sexuality sets up a range of options difficult to negotiate and channel within permanent and enduring relationships.

Postmodern fluidity

For Bauman (2003), relationships and love have become so 'liquid' that there is now a lack of know-how about sustaining long-term relationships. He maintains that personal relationships all too quickly become 'disposable', resulting in an accelerating rate of break-up and termination. The formation of intimate relationships today involves levels of stress and anxiety largely unknown in earlier times. This liquid culture lures people into emotional experimentation, often characterized by fierce intensity, with grossly inflated expectations. Modern consumerism reinforces the intensity as expensive gifts are exchanged, and success is judged by external impressions. Although infatuation has long been a dimension of romantic love, today it makes psychic demands that can be passionate and simultaneously psychologically devastating.

The formation of intimate relationships is also changing rapidly with Internet dating gaining increasing popularity. Sociologists highlight three key features of late postmodern society: *global*, *networked* and *mobile* (cf. Adams 1997; Giddens 1991; Ross 2000) and these features are evident in online dating behavior. The anonymity of the medium, the prevalence of blogs, online photo galleries and personal websites, along with the comfort most of us feel in corresponding entirely through e-mail, have combined to make online dating a perfectly acceptable means of meeting new people. The thrill of not knowing who, when or where you might meet someone is very attractive and sometimes quite addictive. It opens up the constant promise of finding someone, somewhere, and anywhere!

Research indicates that expectations of online dating differ little from off-line practice. Successful outcomes largely depend on the first face-to-face meeting. However, the nature of the medium evokes a type of hyper-communication, with a strong addictive lure. The urge to keep on trying is compelling, as inhibitions drop and the interaction becomes more playful and risky. Even when a permanent and satisfying relationship has been established the temptation to engage with online dating is difficult to resist. Trust and sincerity can be dangerously compromised.

Love's Expansive Culture

In a provocative and inspiring work, popular writer, John Welwood (2007), suggests that all our relational problems arise out of a universal sense of being emotionally wounded, leading to a pursuit of affection that affects not only our personal relationships but the quality of life in our world as a whole. This inner woundedness creates a deep sense that we are not intrinsically lovable just as we are. And this shuts down our capacity to trust, so that even though we may hunger for love, we have difficulty opening to it and letting it circulate freely through us.

The wounding is not just personal and interpersonal. It is in fact transpersonal, and this leads into a much more profound exploration. I suggest the inner pain arises not from some sinful alienation, because of our distance from God, but because of prolonged alienation from the living earth itself. We have not learned how to love creation, so that we can learn how deeply creation loves us. Love is a form of energy, the basis on which all life is begotten, evolves and flourishes. The energy in question is the same life-stuff from which the universe came into being and from which planet Earth evolved (about four billion years ago). The transpersonal aspect of love is cosmic, planetary and personal all at once.

This is not merely an idealistic assertion, understood mystically or philosophically. It is the driving-force that is activating some of the most profound changes in our postmodern understanding of human intimacy. It begins with the recognition that the universal energy is endowed with a deep sense of pattern, forever seeking connection and inter-penetration, an insight science has not yet adopted. According to quantum physics, energy is never wasted; energy connects with other energy forms, ensuing in a process of transformation, which is the life-blood of all-evolutionary becoming.

This same cosmic energy is the attractive propelling force through which people learn to love and form more intimate connections. It becomes particularly embedded in sexual attraction, and in psychosexual intimacy. This is something of a minefield in our modern world, as the sexual repression of many centuries rises up to haunt us with an invasive intensity. For too long we have over-identified sexuality with procreation, thus reducing our sexuality to a biological facility, for the reproduction of the species. Human sexuality should never have been relegated to such a narrow functional purpose, a deviation for which we are now paying a severe penalty.

Psychosexual Intimacy Reclaimed

Human sexuality will look very different in the future. New articulations, with complex challenges, are already transpiring all over the modern world. It feels like sex is back with a vengeance, as wild untamed eroticism explodes all around us. Most people don't understand what is going on, and most are too frightened to ask. Such has been the repression over several centuries, resulting in a subconscious sense of being robbed of erotic empowerment. We want to reclaim a long lost treasure, but we don't know how to go about it. In fact, we are not even sure what the treasure is.

Human sexuality will need a whole new appropriation, as *the sum total of our feelings moods and emotions, articulated through human intimacy.* Sexuality in its primordial meaning is an energy-power connection, relationship, growth and love. It is central to all forms of human bonding, and inevitably leads to bondage when healthy articulation is not possible. It is the human appropriation of the same drive that animates and sustains evolution at every level of life.

The biological reproductive dimension is merely one expression –and relatively insignificant –of a process of psychic energy that defines the essential nature of our human becoming. Our sexuality defines who we are and what evolution wants us to become: creative, relational beings erotically passionate about life, love, and right relating. So much of the conflict in our world, the ravages of war, and the exploitation of other life forms, is in large measure the deviation of a species that has not matured sexually and therefore cannot love proactively.

Reclaiming this more engaging and empowering mode of relational sexuality might well prove to be the most bewildering transition facing our species today. The repressed culture of the past will continue to reap havoc through a great deal of sexual acting-out. Enduring psychosexual commitments will be difficult to honor, the misnamed "fluid" sexuality, identified by several social commentators. Ironically, it is likely to be those who take new sexual liberties –beyond the confines of the biologically determined understanding – who will pave the way to a different future for psychosexual growth.

As sociologist Pitrim Sorokin claimed many years ago, the creative outcomes of major evolutionary shifts tend to be pioneered by the "internal barbarians." I am not suggesting that we recklessly abandon the sexual norms of the past, even when it becomes unambiguously clear that they are outliving their relevance. My concern focuses more on the new sexual ethic we will need, not in the distant future, but very soon. That ethic is unlikely to come from religions or churches, which have lost virtually all credibility when it comes to human sexuality. The new ethic will become the responsibility of social policy makers, with governments having to embrace an ultimate sense of responsibility.

Striving for transparency

Relational transparency is a scarce commodity in the modern world. Millions of people prefer not to think about these deeply personal issues, and subconsciously adopt a stance of business as usual. Another sector explore and experiment as discreetly as possible, succumbing to an unhealthy toxic secrecy. Transparency often ensues in the wake of a crisis, sometimes when a secret affair has been exposed or otherwise comes to light.

Even though popular cultural normalizes a number of new practices, people still do not talk about these issues. In Western countries we have shifted our language from wife/husband to that of partner, and greeting cards for special occasions often use the term *partner* these days. Gay and lesbian issues have come very much into public discourse, yet this is a topic of subdued conversation in several contemporary contexts. Striving to create an adult forum, where adult dialogue can take place, is still a formidable challenge when it comes to issues of intimate human relationships.

In education, there is also a huge lacuna. Attempts in our schools at providing sex education have failed rather dismally. Sex education, I suggest, is primarily a parental responsibility, but sadly one that several parents feel inadequate to carry out. The vacuum is quickly filled by peer-pressure of the youth itself, fed by the voyeurism of our over-sexed culture. The most urgent educational need is the provision of a forum (or forums) where adults can engage in a more adult, enlightened and transparent dialogue on what will remain a major cultural – and personal – issue for many years to come. One can scarcely exaggerate the urgency of this undertaking.

Handling the Transition Wisely

1. Develop a vocabulary to talk intelligently about the transition taking place in human relationships, and in the psychosexual realm today.

2. Make yourself aware of local resources that can assist and support people negotiating difficulties in their relationships.

3. Explore rituals for relational commitments, but also for painful endings to short or long term relationships.

4. Can you with a trusted friend, work colleague, or counselor, share your feelings about the amorphous sexual landscape described in this Section?

5. If the opportunity arises, engage public representatives with the challenge of developing a new sexual ethic for our time.

6. Spiritually, can you embrace the notion that eroticism is a primary divine characteristic?

19. *What does Critical Thinking Look Like in the Twenty-first Century?*

Every negative thought I entertain in my head, which I think is my own secret place, actually strengthens the negative field that sweeps our world. Every time I bemoan the negative world out there that I must suffer, I have supported and contributed to it through my moaning. My secret place in my head is not so secret after all.

Joseph Chilton Pearce.

Educational systems throughout the world heavily emphasize passive learning, obedience to legitimate authority, and respect for those senior to you. A tendency to disagree, verbalize alternative viewpoints, or question legitimate authority, not merely elicits disapproval, but frequently results in disciplinary action. Thus the child from a young age internalizes the key values of our predominantly patriarchal culture, amid several salient pressures to perpetuate the inherited power system.

It is a highly successful strategy that has produced many of the benefits we enjoy in modern society. However, it has left us with several liabilities: might is right; those at the top know best; win at any cost; play the power game to your advantage; power and wealth go together; people are superior to every other life-form; war is necessary for peace; there is no room for vulnerability; women are inferior to men. Those who opt for a more non-violent, cooperative, sustainable way of living, more sensitive to the needs of the rest of creation, tend to be dismissed as misguided freaks. Those who think for themselves and raise critical questions are perceived as a threat to be subdued and when possible suppressed.

Because we live in an information-saturated age, the capacity for curiosity and critical reflection has increased exponentially. There is a significant decrease in those who look to higher authority for the definitive truth. We see a rapid rise in suspicion and disagreement. People explore views and opinions through multi-media outlets before approaching a specialist. The capacity for critical appraisal is a feature of our time, which as yet has not received the attention it merits.

Lateral Thinking

The shift towards a more critical consciousness has been in the making throughout the closing decades of the twentieth century. A useful example is the popularity of entrepreneur, Edward de Bono and his novel idea of *lateral thinking* (de Bono 1970; 1992). Several cultural assumptions are called into question particularly the favored patriarchal mode of rational thought, logical analysis, and deductive reasoning. The linear chain of cause-and-effect gives way to the quantum leap that embraces uncertainty and non-linearity. Imagination is prized more highly than cold rational logic.

These are a few of de Bono's working principles, inviting us to embrace the lateral way of engaging with our world:

1. *Match your thinking with your perceptions*! In the world of rational, logical discourse, we work with a range of assumptions, somewhat similar to playing a game of chess that starts out with a set of given pieces. But what are those pieces? In most real life situations the pieces are not given, we just assume they are there. We embrace inherited perceptions, with accompanying concepts and presupposed boundaries. Lateral thinking is concerned not with playing with the existing pieces but with seeking to change those very pieces. In real life experience, very few things are fixed or subject to rigid homogeneity. Rather everything is fluid, open, creative and amenable to imaginative reconstruction.

2. *We live in a self-organizing universe*, and our psyches are tuned to appropriate that creative process. The human brain is not a mechanical product but rather an informationally aligned system with a mathematical need for moving across patterns, seeking out optimal creativity. The tools and processes of lateral thinking are designed to achieve such enriching complexity. The tools are based on an understanding of self-organizing information systems, with the universe itself providing the foundational models.

3. *Creativity is our default position*, which linear thought processes often neglect and undermine. In our predominantly patriarchal cultures, we have been indoctrinated to opt for conventional linear modes, which encourages sameness, blandness, homogeneity, and sequential continuity; with strong emphasis on fidelity to the orders given by those who govern from the top down. Lateral thought seeks

out the relationships that enhance creativity and welcomes complexity.

The lateral approach is captivated in the following words of Margaret J. Wheatley, an organizational consultant who radically changed her working strategies after embracing the insights of quantum physics. She writes:

> My growing sensibility of a quantum universe has affected my organizational life in several ways. First, I try hard to discipline myself to remain aware of the whole and to resist my well-trained desire to analyze the parts to death. I look now for patterns of movement over time and focus on qualities like rhythm, flow, direction, and shape. Second, I know I am wasting time whenever I draw straight arrows between two variables in a cause and effect diagram, or position things as polarities, or create elaborate plans and time lines. Third, I no longer argue with anyone about what is real. Fourth, the time I formerly spent on detailed planning and analysis I now use to look at the structures that might facilitate relationships. I have come to expect that something useful occurs if I link up people, units, or tasks, even though I cannot determine precise outcomes. And last, I realize more and more that the universe will not cooperate with my desires for determinism. Wheatley (1992, 43-44).

Not merely is this a different way of viewing the world, and our engagement with daily living. It also involves an internal shift moving many people towards a different sense of self-identity. Initially dislocating, and sometimes confusing, it moves us towards greater self-reliance and self-confidence, a development that several major institutions do not easily embrace. This novel identity marks the emergence of a new quality of being adult in our time. It is an evolving process, with a potential yet to be named and explored.

The new sense of being adult

In former times adulthood was identified as a life-stage initiated around one's eighteenth birthday with the right to vote, the beginning of formal training for a career, the maturity to move towards a monogamous relationship culminating in marriage, the establishment of a home, and the procreation of a new family. Thus the dominant culture could point to a list of achievements constituting the mature adult, the responsible citizen capable of serving the State and God in a fruitful manner.

Today, we judge adulthood more in terms of forming a range of relationships across several aspects of life, including developmental growth, personal relationships, education, work – all of which are considered to be life-long processes rather than once-off achievements. In this ambience, the key features of being adult include flexibility, adaptability, creativity, openness to process, a sense of organicity with the entire web of life, and a spiritual sense of affiliation with the cosmic creation itself.

It leaves many people reeling with confusion, but increasingly we are adjusting to a new way of being, which has yet to establish its cultural and human credibility in our world. And this new adult human tends to question everything, frequently at a loss on where to turn to obtain an informed and enlightened response.

Theoretically, our educational systems acknowledge this new adulthood, and several webpages describe the strategies conducive to adult formation and education. In the past the mature adult was judged by unquestioned fidelity to those in charge, and learned by passive acquiescence of inherited wisdom. Now the new adult is encouraged to question, to criticize, to imagine in a more lateral fashion, and, collaboratively, to explore more creative ways of engaging with life. Thus the learning process is meant to be more interactive and dynamic. It veers towards multidisciplinary analyses of life-situations, and supporting interdisciplinary engagement with every aspect of our experience.

The theory is impressive, and makes sense in terms of the evolutionary consciousness characterizing our time. Sadly, many of those developing the theory – especially our academics – have not themselves undergone the consciousness shift, leaving us with a gaping credibility gap.

Attending to conscious thought

The study of consciousness is one of the most exciting and empowering developments of recent decades. Despite the fact that academics, for the greater part, adopt Daniel Dennett's rather mechanistic understanding – namely, that consciousness is nothing more than an accumulation of tiny objects (called qualia) in the human brain (Dennett 1993) – there is a growing body of creative thinkers exploring a range of other models. Of particular interest to the present work is the notion that consciousness belongs primarily to the cosmic realm (the entire universe) and we, humans, appropriate our capacity for consciousness from that creative cosmic source. (More in van Lommel 2011).

This enlarged understanding alerts us to the nature and power of human thought. Endowed with *holographic brains* (itself a controversial topic – see webpage: http://en.wikipedia. org/wiki/Holonomic_brain_theory), every thought we entertain is a form of energy entwined with the creative vitality of the universe itself. What we do with our thoughts has far-reaching consequence, the nature of which we are only beginning to understand. Several studies have been done on this subject, and for a valuable resume I recommend the research of the British futurist, Lynn McTaggart (2007).

Since every thought is a form of energy it goes somewhere and does something. There is no such thing as a passing thought. Although humans have not much control over their thought processes, we can make significant choices related to both the quality and quantity of our thinking, which in this case also includes our perceptions. Several studies have highlighted the potential of positive thinking, such as desiring healing for a sick person, or reinforcing the possibility of more empowering outcomes. By the same token, negative thought patterns can disrupt and undermine the flow of creative energy.

Human conversation is an example worth considering. Every time I praise and complement another person I enhance the potential of their field of creativity. We all know from experience the power of positive strokes. We are less vigilant on the impact of negative energy. Every time I criticize an organization, e.g., a government agency or a religious institution, the chances are that I am bolstering up its negative power. The energy of my criticism actually reinforces the destructive potential of the organization; inadvertently I am giving energy to the very thing I am criticizing, and therefore I am enhancing a destructive rather than a fruitful outcome. If I want to withdraw energy from the organization, then the more responsible thing to do would be to say nothing. Spare the energy I would have invested in my criticism and, instead invest it in dreaming up alternatives to the organization's negative way of behaving. (More in Chilton Pearce 2002, 80ff).

I suspect many people have thought about this, but the suggestion is so subversive and counter-intuitive, that few people act accordingly. It takes a great deal of self-awareness, and spiritual vigilance, to behave in this way. There is also a very fine line between a constructive critique, and a criticism that is likely to be counterproductive. Scripture scholar, Walter Brueggemann, reflecting on the prophetic counter-culture of the Hebrew Scriptures, claims that an in-depth critique automatically instigates more energizing ways for behaving constructively. In his words, we criticize in order to energize. We consciously choose thoughts and words with transformation as the desired goal.

Our thought-forms not merely influence, they can actually transform. And our words need to be congruent with our thoughts and the desires underpinning our motivation. Language is a form of energy, and will energize for weal or for woe. Our dominant political systems are very skillful at employing forms of rhetoric that baffle and bemuse the general public. Particularly at election times, people are lured by promises that are blatantly false, and incapable of being fulfilled. Many people recognize this; yet subconsciously collude with the veneer of hope that something good might come from the impressive rhetoric. Once again, humanity finds itself in this confusing in-between evolutionary time in which we know intuitively that the familiar world of yester-years is falling apart. Yet, frightened by the prospect of a vacuum, we continue to support that which we know can offer us no realistic hope for the future. Not a nice place to be!

Action follows thought

Our dominant culture tends to judge success by external achievement. Everything is externalized, even our thought-energy. We waste a great deal of creative energy in a range of cultural projections that evoke in us frustration and estrangement when our goals are not realized (most of the time), and a deluded sense of satisfaction when our aspirations are fulfilled. In other words, we respond more like passive children rather than creatively critical adults. In this co-dependent condition, our thought-energy supports several dysfunctional ways of being.

We cannot recall too often the scholastic dictum: *action follows thought*. As we think, so we act! If we want to change action, we need to change thought-patterns first. (Some times, of course, it takes changed action to alter our ways for seeing and understanding). What exactly does this the principle mean and how do we mobilize its empowering wisdom? Our patriarchal, industrial and technological cultures are fundamentally geared towards external achievement, and evaluate their success by quantifiable results. In our work, we are hired because of our ability to perform specific tasks, and we are rewarded (paid) on the merit of being able to deliver the goods at the end of the process. How meaningful the process is to both actor and receiver, how internally congruent it feels, or how much human fulfillment it releases, are all seen as secondary consequences, and in some cases are viewed as superficial distractions.

The mechanistic nature of work in the industrial and technological spheres is well known and is the basis of Herbert Marcuse's label of the one-dimensional man. Paradoxically, it is the information explosion –and its accompanying computer technology - that is evoking a new work ethic rich in multi-dimensional potential. And this new complexity is also evoking more critical ways of seeing and thinking, although still only at a peripheral level.

For humanity at his time we stand on a critical threshold, with a rather grim future facing us. (This is the subject of our next section.) To engage in more frenzied activity, compulsive achievement, or to be so driven, is not likely to be of much use as we face this impending crisis. Inner resourcefulness rather than external attainment is likely to be crucial. Many protagonists highlight the need for a new spiritual acumen (as explored in Section 29 below), but not many have alerted us to the psychic dimension (our perceptual and thought energy). Without this fresh lateral and critical mindset, we are unlikely to embrace the new spiritual conversion. Mind and spirit are psychic bedfellows; both need our considered and discerning attention at this critical juncture in our human and earthly evolution.

Handling the Transition Wisely:

1. What life-changes can you make to become a more critically reflective person?

2. Are there groups or organizations you could join that would help to heighten your critical awareness?

3. Are there fears in your life that at times inhibit your creative imagination; what do you need to do to outgrow them?

4. Are you clear on the difference between criticism and critiquing?

5. Where do you stand with the integration of mind and spirit in your personal growth and development?

6. Do you have soul mates who challenge and inspire you to reflect more deeply?

20. *Humans on the brink of Extinction*

For each of the Big Five (extinctions) there are theories of what caused them, some of them compelling but none proven. For the sixth extinction, however, we do know the culprit. We are!

Richard Leakey & Roger Lewin (1996).

Many of the reflections in Part Two of this book relate to the human predicament we observe today: fierce competition, mass disempowerment, and disillusionment with many of the major institutions we encounter in daily life. There is a non-human issue that is also approaching a critical realization, and that is the state of the living earth itself: accelerating climate change; environmental degradation; diminishing oil, water, forests, and arable land; and growing economic instability generated by global capitalism. In such a wounded earth-body, humans stand no chance of living meaningfully if indeed living at all. This adds to our human alienation, precisely because we are so ambivalent about what we ourselves have done and continue to do to exacerbate the problem.

Various experts pronounce differently on the gravity of our situation. The grimmest scenario, described by Leakey and Lewin (1996), claims that our plight is irreversible and that *Homo Sapiens* itself is in fact *the sixth major extinction*. Such is our exploitation of the earth's natural resources, and the compulsive arrogance with which we pursue such reckless meddling, that it will be impossible to reverse the degradation and havoc we have caused. More disturbingly, there is little evidence to suggest that humans want to reverse the destruction. We enjoy the "benefits" too much.

A difficult discernment

Who is in the right here: the alarmists or those who pursue business as usual? In truth, very few are in total denial of the urgent and precarious state of affairs. What prevails may be described as a "pseudo-blindness" that runs something like this: "Yes, things have gone badly out of kilter, and the future does not look good for humanity, but we are a species with a strange sense of resilience, and we seem to have survived previous crises of global proportion, so let's not lose hope entirely." Additionally there are those – perhaps of a more fundamentalist persuasion - who invest faith in a divine omnipotent force, capable of rescuing humanity from its own perdition as allegedly God has often done in former times.

Increasingly, the religious argument cuts little ice, even for devoted religionists themselves. It invokes a God of the gaps, who is rapidly losing favor in virtually every realm of human life. The cultural-historical argument requires a more informed and nuanced critique. In our long history, of seven million years, humans have endured several major crises, many involving large-scale extinction of various life forms. In some cases, it looks like the prevailing humans of the day, e.g., the Neanderthals, died out. Yet, the human species re-invented itself and sprang forth afresh.

Here, in all probability, we are encountering the great cosmic and planetary paradox of birth-death-rebirth. New life always seems to require significant destruction of what previously prevailed. It happens at every level of evolution, including our human story. To the human eye it looks capricious and even bizarre, and certainly puts pay to any sense of an all-powerful controlling God. We are dealing with a paradox that defies rational and religious explanation; nonetheless a paradoxical element without which all creation will come to naught.

Is our present ecological crisis one of nature's paradoxical moments, or is it humanly instigated without any sense of evolutionary timeliness? This is the baffling question for which there is not an obvious answer. And I suspect on previous occasions, it was only after the paradoxical crisis had transpired, that humans could name and identify what had actually taken place.

At every moment in evolution, including the procession of human affairs, death and new birth is taking place. Everybody wants to embrace the birth, but nobody wants to engage with death and mortality. *It is our denial of death more than anything else that inhibits our potential for wise and informed discernment at this precarious time.* On the one hand, we need to name and embrace that which belongs to the past and to which we should no longer cling on, e.g., our prevailing capitalistic financial system which benefits only a human minority, and exerts a heavy toll on the earth's eco-system. On the other hand, in our compulsive craving for the new, we recklessly dump inherited truths that still serve a useful and empowering purpose, e.g., the organic dynamics of the living earth, best known to many of our indigenous peoples around the world. In both cases, we ask the obvious question: what prevents us from seeing and acting in more enlightened ways?

Whither the counter-cultural?

On closer analysis, it is not difficult to see where the resistance lies, and who are those blocking more sane and informed ways of moving forward. It is those who command the high ground of power, wealth and control who are holding us all to ransom. The survival of the fittest is in fact the pathway to annihilation. It eventually destroys even the powerful. On the one-hand, our economics is compulsively driven for gain and profit to benefit primarily those who already have more than they need. On the other hand, it is those same predators who will not entertain consideration of indigenous wisdom and alternative ways of using the earth's resources.

What is the solution? The cruel irony facing us is that most of us don't want to ask that question because it would demand of us an involvement that would disturb and threaten our comfort zones. It is not easy to walk away from dysfunctional relationships: whether in our marriages, our homes, or workplaces, or our churches. "Try and change the situation from within" is a favored response, but at critically evolutionary crossroads where we seem to be at today, that strategy is seen to be inadequate by I ncreasing numbers of people. Working for an alternative is the more authentic option, although often a risky undertaking. In the process, one is likely to lose many previous securities, and once one embraces the new endeavor, it is difficult to return to what previously worked to one's advantage.

Our hope is invested primarily in the shift of consciousness taking place around the world. More and more people realize that the standard patriarchal way of behaving is dysfunctional and unsustainable. Intuitively, more people know it cannot last, and will not last. There is an accompanying shift in awareness that a good quality of human life is impossible without a radical shift in how we relate with the earth — ecologically and environmentally. We cannot go on exploiting indiscriminately. Not merely are there limits to what we can take from the web of life, but an informed sense of give-and-take is essential to our health and wellbeing, as well as to our dignity and sense of meaning in the world.

The notion of a counter-culture has been to the fore since the 1960s. Perhaps it needed all that time to strike root, and it looks as if it will need more time, but certainly not an indefinite period. Ironically, the authenticity of the shift may be gauged by the panic reactions of the early twenty-first century: a number of European governments tried to ban alternative health systems in favor of conventional medicine; the Catholic church imposed a revived Latinism in the language of liturgy to counter the tendency towards greater fluidity and flexibility; massive debt bail-outs were required to keep a faltering capitalistic system on its feet. In all cases, the invasive threat of another way of doing business - a counter-cultural alternative – was staved off, in a compulsively driven desire to retain a veneer of normalcy. There are unambiguous indications that the counter-culture is coming of age. But it is being met with fierce resistance from the dominant culture.

International conferences on climate change highlight a grave and urgent issue. We continue to quibble about scientific procedure, while the negative impact continues to increase. Perhaps, the crisis has to deepen further before we become proactive, and for some it will then be too late, especially for the poor and disenfranchised. It is a classical, messy in-between space, and it will take enormous courage and vision even to stay with the untidy process. For those among us trying to hold on to some semblance of integrity, the painful choices become clearer by the day. However, millions live with the impending fear: are all our efforts too little too late!

Will we make it through?

Humanity has survived many evolutionary crises. Our chances of surviving this one are quite high. But there will be a price to pay, and it will make heavy demands on human viability. A human catastrophe of unimaginable proportions is likely to occur sometime in the twenty-first century. It is unlikely to be a nuclear attack, although it remains a continual threat. It is more likely to be an environmental crisis within the earth-body itself, as the biochemistry of the planet becomes incapable of sustaining human life, as we know it today.

Millions of human casualties will ensue, and it may impact upon other life forms as well, although those other forms are likely to exhibit resilience unknown to us humans. This catastrophe will be the creative paradox, without which we are unlikely to make the adjustments necessary to live in a more benign, sustainable, and ecologically connected way.

If this grim scenario is to come through, what then is the point in writing, talking, or thinking about it? I suspect it will be those among us, who can entertain and befriend this frightening prospect, who will serve as catalysts for the transformative challenge of the newly evolving future. We may lose our lives in the daring endeavor, but our raised awareness – even in death – will enhance the evolutionary shift whereby some will make it across and become the protagonists of a new tomorrow.

In Christian language, I am describing the spirituality of the paschal journey, the paradox that required the historical Jesus to undergo a painful (and meaningless) death before the transformative experience known as Resurrection. It is that same paradox that characterizes our human experience at several moments of our life journey: we die to the small self in order to give way to a greater realization. It is the basis of many moments popularly described as life-crises.

That personal sense of crisis and paradox is an appropriation of a universal process that has characterized evolution from the dawn of time. Death gives way to new life, and without the death of the old, we cannot embrace the novel breakthroughs that evolution require for the creative and complex creation we inhabit. We belong to an unfolding story greater than ourselves, one that is not alien to our nature and its becoming, but one that does involve evolutionary leaps that are as daunting as they are promising, demanding as they are liberating.

To assist us in our forward journey, I explore in Part Three of this book some of the breakthroughs evolution seems to be activating at this critical cultural juncture of our lives. If we can learn to flow with these emerging possibilities then we stand a better chance of being proactive beneficiaries of the breakthrough rather than passive victims of the breakdown. And in this engagement, we encounter a sense of hope with significant spiritual import for the twenty-first century.

Handling the Transition Wisely

1. Are you fearful about the future of Planet Earth; can you name your greatest fears?

2. What are your fears around your own personal mortality – and with whom do you share them?

3. What life-changes can you make to live in a more sustainable way?

4. How aware are you of the resources of your local bioregion?

5. How comfortable are you in regarding the natural world as a living subject, rather than an object for human use?

6. Name some of the ingredients for empowering spirituality to sustain us during this time of uncertain evolutionary breakthrough.

Third Benchmark: *Chaos and the Creative Lure of the Future*

Nobody likes too much chaos. It threatens our security and undermines our well-indoctrinated minds that we are in charge of our world and should be able to control its destiny. And for so long religion, politics, and economics fostered order and harmony. It seems that God does not like chaos, and neither should we.

Christianity is not the only religion to suggest that creation itself was born out of chaos, and in the closing decades of the twentieth century, scientists gave chaos a new terminology. Psychologists and psychotherapists encouraged us to befriend chaos instead of trying to eliminate it. The mystics have long encouraged us to embrace the dark night of the soul and the dark night of the senses – and not simply try to dodge or avoid them.

It is easier to engage the dark when we have some glimpse of a light at the end of the tunnel. Spirituality of all the great traditions lists hope as a necessary supplement for faith. Even in the Old Testament Book of Job, in which a rather cruel demanding God is stripping Job of every certainty and achievement of his existence, God keeps reminding Job of the wonder and elegance of the creation that surrounds him. That for Job seems to be the light at the end of the tunnel providing some semblance of hope in the midst of his terrible despair.

Fractal mathematics (http://en.wikipedia.org/wiki/Fractal) graphically illustrates the deep order that lies hidden within and beneath the observable layers of chaos and confusion. With these elaborate computer simulations, we can unravel deep patterns within external irregularity and turbulence. The Spirit who breathes order into creation, according to the book of Genesis, may also be revisioned as the creative cosmic force forever seeking to draw forth creativity from the primal unformed depths. At every level of creation, hope holds an ultimate-ness we must never abandon.

The reflections in Part Three of this book evoke this primal and primordial sense of hope. Evolution seems to include a preferred sense of direction, which Teilhard de Chardin named as growth into greater complexity. As things move along, life is enriched and enhanced – with what I will venture to call *a greater sense of purpose*. To grasp this insight we may need to clear away a lot of the complicated clutter that surrounds the notion of evolution itself.

In its essential meaning, evolution describes an unfolding process with three central features: *growth - change - development.* And we witness the process at every level of life from the microcosmic realm of the subatomic domain to the vast galactic spheres glimpsed through the sophisticated space-telescopes of recent times. Even a child r can understand the meaning of the three words (growth, change, development), yet the evolutionary significance is highly nuanced and its core meaning quite complex.

GROWTH: In organic terms growth always involves paradox, the baffling intermingling of creation-*cum*-destruction. The young plant evolves from a highly complex process of the seed decaying and dying, transforming many times and embracing a range of stages which in botanical terms are easily named but not fully understood. In the organic world, including the emergence of the human being, growth is a complex process that defies rational and scientific explanation in several of its key features.

CHANGE: External change is easy to observe, measure, quantify and, to an extent, control. Internally, it is impossible to figure out what is transpiring, largely because of unpredictabilities and a range of factors inaccessible to human observation. More baffling still are the dynamics of quantum physics, which affect every life form at the microcosmic level, with an impact so open-ended and unpredictable that several scientists choose not to explore or investigate.

DEVELOPMENT: This is not merely another word for growth, nor can it be reduced to a sequence of fairly well understood stages of emergence into a fully developed organism, whether human, plant or bacterium. In neo-Darwinian terms, development is assumed as a linear unfolding from past to present and onto a future which will be shaped and determined because of past influences. Central to this process is the popularized notion of *the survival of the fittest*, in which less resilient forms are weeded out, while the stronger and more useful survive.

The controlling influence of the past carries dogmatic weight in both science and religion. An authentic future cannot be anything other than what the past produced, and which has proved to have an enduring value. Process thinkers, philosophically and religiously, have consistently questioned the foundations of this perception. Instead, they postulate a "lure of the future" which also influences development, to a degree that most researchers are reluctant to accept.

The lure of the future sounds dangerously close to some kind of esoteric speculation, and will not be taken seriously by most scholars. Only those acquainted with a multi-disciplinary approach are likely to give it serious consideration. John F. Haught (2000; 2010) of Georgetown University (USA) highlights its significance adopting both biological and religious insights. Stated in simple terms the argument goes like this: The future is not merely a chance outcome largely dependent on what has gone before. Rather, there exists in the created order (at cosmic and planetary levels) a deep internal wisdom, named by the scientist, David Bohm, as the implicate order. It may be understood as a dimension of the capacity for self-organization (*autopoiesis*), which flourishes throughout all creation. This wisdom arises not merely from the accumulated achievements of the past (the neo-

Darwinian understanding), but also acts like a force of attraction, pulling evolutionary growth towards creative future possibilities. For John Haught, this lure of the future may be *the* major factor at work in all evolutionary unfolding.

In religious terms, this insight belongs more to mysticism rather than to religion in its popular meaning. Mystics have flourished in all cultures and religions, and are widely regarded as mavericks that do not easily fit within conventional boundaries. They are often deemed to be suspect and frequently denounced as heretical. In mystical understanding, it is the living Spirit of God who instigates and sustains the lure of the future, drawing everything in a *forward* movement toward the potential for richer form and more creative expression, because newness and creativity are deemed to be central features of divine life itself.

Evolutionary creativity –whether viewed from a human or divine perspective cannot be contained, unified and controlled merely in terms of what we have inherited from the past. It is open to a new future, and carries within its trajectory a lure for novel form and expression. It is the lure of that open-ended future that preoccupies us in Part Three of this book.

Part Three:

THE EVOLUTIONARY LURE OF THE FUTURE

Anticipation is what bears the universe along as it reaches out toward fuller being.

John F. Haught

It is our imagination that allows us to give form to the Spirit's urgings.

Judy Cannato

21. The Quantum Lure of the Future

Be alert for the Lure of a mystical complex worldview which neither rational science nor formal religion can resist any longer

What we have gained by controlling the world as a collection of objects, we have lost in our capacity for intimacy in the communion of subjects.

Thomas Berry.

In the closing decades of the twentieth century, our way of viewing the world, and our place in it, changed dramatically. Some attribute the new awareness to the information explosion, others to the impact of mass media and more international travel, while others pointed to scientific breakthroughs that forced us to question several prevailing theories and assumptions.

Although it initially transpired in the opening decades of the twentieth century, the radical and controversial vision of *Quantum Theory* only impacted on a global scale from around 1970 onwards. The landing on the moon in 1969, along with major developments in computer science in the 1970s, inaugurated a new scientific consciousness, with an increasing number of writers describing the shift from classic science to quantum physics, from the scientific metaphor of the Machine to that of the Holon. A more intricate and mysterious way of viewing the world was coming into its own, with an allurement and fascination that gripped the imagination of millions – and still does.

The Quantum Leap

In a previous work (O'Murchu 2004), I explore some of the social and spiritual implications of the quantum revolution. For the present work, I adopt a more poetic approach to tantalize and evoke the creative imagination. Take a moment to ponder the following statements:

1. Every breath you take contains an atom breathed out by the Buddha.

2. You age faster at the top of a building rather than at the bottom.

3. An atom can be in many different places at once, the equivalent of you being in New York and Singapore at the same time.

4. One per cent of the static on a television tuned between stations is a relic of the Big Bang.

5. A cup of coffee weighs more when hot than cold.

6. There is a liquid that can run uphill.

7. The faster you travel, the slimmer you get.

8. The entire human race would fit in the volume of a sugar cube.

These statements introduce us to the enigmatic world of quantum physics. In fact, they are a more direct way to understanding the perplexities of the quantum worldview, which suggests that life functions at two levels: the *overt, cause-and-effect* realm of experience as distinct from the *covert, implicate, microcosmic* domain where things happen in real but very strange ways. In the quantum domain, all the above statements are *true* – leaving us with several tantalizing questions: What is truth? And how do we detect truthfulness? How do we perceive the true meaning of reality?

As we move into a perplexing and uncertain future, we all have to grapple with one of the most fundamental questions of all time: what is the real world? What is reality? Am I suggesting that our senses always deceive us? No, I am not. Rather I am proposing, as the quantum worldview does, that we have been trained to perceive and understand our world in a rational, mechanistic, cause-and-effect manner which is proving to be increasingly unreliable, superficial, and problematic in a range of significant ways. Our dominant perceptions are valuable and functional but often leave the human heart aching for something we know to be different and more real.

Quantum mechanics has bequeathed to us the many blessings of science and technology. But paradoxically, it is that same progressive wisdom that is reaping havoc on the planet and its natural resources, leaving us with a rather apocalyptic diagnosis for the future of human life on earth (cf. Section 20 above). All of which is pushing the collective consciousness to ask: "Is the inherited paradigm just inadequate, or it is actually down right false, and therefore creating a road to nowhere?"

The choice . . .

The twenty-first century may well be remembered as the one in which humanity chose violence over peace, destruction over progress, death over life. It is as real – and as grim – as that. Our conventional ways of being – personally, socially, politically and economically – are increasingly seen to be dysfunctional and counter-productive. As the crisis deepens, more people are seeking a different way ahead. We evidence around us a widespread sense of weariness, an ennui, which millions seek to escape through the hedonistic allurements of our popular culture, while many others rationalize their predicament, fiercely devoted to making money and building earthly empires.

The millions who are now choosing to seek out an alternative counter-culture are not sure what they desire. Intuitively and often confusedly, they know it has to be different from what they already experience in daily life. The quantum worldview is winning out, embroiling us in tantalizing questions, which we know will not go away. A new consciousness, a more expansive sense of awareness, is catching up on us. We are beginning to see and understand according to a changing logic; it is only a matter of time until evolution will also compel us to act differently.

Action tends to follow thought. So firstly, there has to be *a shift in consciousness*, and today our awareness levels have been elevated sharply. Consciousness itself has been closely aligned with the quantum worldview (as I indicate in the next Section). Indeed, one cannot hope to grasp what quantum mechanics is about without a radical change in perception and comprehension. A whole new mind-set is needed.

The encouraging thing is that this new mind-set is catching up on humanity. Millions know that alternatives are possible and millions want to engage with other ways of relating to our world. How to go about it is the big dilemma, particularly with so much to lose by way of power, control and comfort.

The holistic vision at the heart of the quantum theory will eventually catch up with humanity. Evolution will push us into a new way of seeing, and novel ways of being. Like most major evolutionary shifts it will be costly, and may well involve an extinction-type crisis, the likes of which we evidenced in earlier evolutionary transitions (cf. Section 20 above). The degree to which humans will survive the crisis will only be manifest after the event.

The lure . . .

In fact survival may not be the appropriate concern. Our preoccupation with survival may in itself be a major cultural block. It may be more responsible to conceive how we go through the crisis even if we lose our lives in the process. The fear of mass extinction can easily distract us from the more urgent – and adult – consideration: how do we die with dignity? This is a difficult question for our species; so effective are we at rationalizing death in our world. We dread death, we deny it and we constantly flee from it. This may well be the reason why we have so much meaningless death in the world today.

It is easier to befriend the death-process when we realize that we cannot - and do not - control the process of evolution.

The popular neo-Darwinian view sees evolution at every level as driven from the past; those forms that proved good at survival in the past are likely to be the ones that will carry us into the future. The past determines the future.

This linear, logical understanding has been challenged by a number of visionary scholars (quantum thinkers) in the closing decades of the twentieth century. I have already alluded to the seminal work of John F. Haught, of Georgetown university (USA), who claims that the neo-Darwinian notion of evolution being driven from behind provides, at best, only a partial explanation of how we understand the evolutionary process; the other dimension consists of what he calls *the lure of the future* (Haught 2000; 2010). Evolution not merely pushes from the past; it also draws us towards a desired future. We are lured into future-oriented possibilities, and we don't have much choice but to follow, even though we do not know where exactly we are being led. Those that resist the lure lose out, and become extinct.

The reader may be quick to accuse me of irrational determinism, which is what it looks like from a rational point of view, whether scientifically or religiously substantiated. The lure of the future cannot be analyzed rationally, no more than the quantum worldview can be. And it is premature to dismiss it as an esoteric "new-age" wild fantasy. The lure has a strong spiritual underpinning, for which I suggest mysticism, rather than formal religion, may provide the interpretative clues.

On closer reflection, we are lured by the future every moment of our lives. It is our dreams, ambitions, desires and hopes that drive our daily activity. We work and earn money in order to build a better home, raise a more successful family, and promote a more flourishing business. The future not merely informs every now; it motivates and gives our lives a sense of direction and purpose. That which gives meaning to daily life, is the energy motivated by the future that lies before us. The future is the primary driving force in our daily lives.

And the same is true of the process of evolution itself, which is difficult to accept and believe because we have for so long conceptualized it in an excessively cerebral and functional way. Now linear thinking needs to give way to lateral visioning. The rationalist must give way to the mystic. This brings us to the threshold of a new consciousness engaging many creative thinkers at this time. To that topic we now turn our attention.

22. *Consciousness Drives Change*

Be Alert to the Lure of expansive ways of seeing and understanding shaking the metaphysical foundations we trusted for so long.

Consciousness should be viewed as an emergent product of a sequence of self-organizing processes that form part of a general advance of complexity occurring throughout the universe.

Paul W. Davies.

Consciousness is a recurring theme throughout the pages of this book. I have already alluded to work of Daniel Dennett (1992) for whom consciousness consists of a mechanism at work in the human brain propelling the units of consciousness (qualia) to do their work. Among academics and professional scientists this is the most widely accepted view of consciousness. It is a dimension of human awareness, a mechanistic process operative only in the human brain.

At the other end of the spectrum is the view advocated by David Chalmers (1996) and by a number of other pioneering theorists —some scientists, others psychologists —that consciousness belongs first and foremost to the cosmic creation, and that humans appropriate it from the universe mediated through our embedded-ness in the living earth. Thus writes Pim van Lommel, a proponent of this view:

> Consciousness has a primary presence in the universe, and all matter possesses subjective properties or consciousness. In this view, consciousness is non-local and the origin or foundation of everything: all matter, or physical reality, is shaped by non-local consciousness. There is no longer any distinction between non-local space and consciousness. This is not a new insight. As far back as the seventeenth century, Newton held that the omnipresent space might be filled with a "spiritual substance"; he called space the "divine observatory."(van Lommel 2010, 248).

Like many protagonists of this expansive view, van Lommel borrows heavily from quantum theory to defend this alternative understanding. Congruent with the enlarged worldview which appeals to a growing body of people in our time, I am proposing that this awakening of global consciousness – along with the trans-mechanistic understanding of what it is – is luring humanity into a new evolutionary leap. It may be one of those emergent possibilities that occurs only once in every several thousand years. It is big stuff, and its propensity for empowering change is enormous.

Mind over Matter

We associate consciousness with the power of mind. This notion of the mind being more foundational than matter has been a popular idea for well over a hundred years now. However, consciousness should not be identified merely with our mental functions of thought and perception. It signifies much more than that. Consciousness is better described as *a psychic giftedness*, an inner driving force that animates and energizes from within – the universe, planet earth, the person, and each bacterium. And it is one and the same consciousness that endows all created reality.

What is the source of consciousness? Who or what created it? The major religions postulate God as the original creator of all that exists. My sense is that we are dealing with something more profound and ancient than any and all religious insight. Consciousness is one of those emergent properties that arises – and flourishes – when creativity is flowing. It is the wisdom within all living, evolving processes, rather than anything introduced by an external fabricator, divine or otherwise. It is a central feature of the within-ness of everything, ultra real, yet incapable of human measurement or manipulation.

It operates within the energy that undergirds all created form, something similar to the ill-fated ether of classical science. It is energetic but cannot be reduced to any of the human strategies for measuring energy. In another book, I describe the universal energy as a central feature of what indigenous peoples describe as the Great Spirit (O'Murchu 2012). The notion of Great Spirit must not be confused with God as described in mainstream religion. God has several anthropocentric features and at least in the monotheistic faiths (Judaism, Christianity and Islam) is often described as personal. The Great Spirit is a transpersonal life force, the primary source of the creativity, which gives birth to, and sustains, everything in creation.

Consciousness certainly has close associations with cosmic energy, creativity and Great Spirit. But it should not be identified exclusively with any one element. It defies precise categorization. Our inability to subject it to scientific clarity – like the quantum theory itself – may, in fact, be the "mystical" outcome best suited to our ongoing investigation of this indefinable but enduring phenomenon. Many of the great mystics seem to be grounded in an experiential sense of cosmic consciousness, a deep sense of sacredness pervading all reality. They seem reluctant to say much more about it, and I guess it would be wise for us to support their intuitive reticence.

Jungian psychology also has a take on this cosmic consciousness. Carl Jung envisaged the wisdom of quantum physics as an endorsement for the existence of what he named as the collective unconscious (Collected Works, Vol.9, 412). It is an unfortunate choice of words, chosen to describe an all-embracing energetic field-force, sustaining everything in being and conferring on the created world the propensity for evolutionary growth. Jung traces its origin to the Divine Life permeating everything in creation.

In humans, the collective unconscious impacts upon all behavior, consciously and subconsciously. It is the amalgam of all the thoughts, feelings, aspirations and ideas that have ever been experienced. It is a reservoir of spiritual, psychic, and mental energy, and it exists everywhere. We cannot escape its influence. We cannot change its past, but we can contribute to its future unfolding. In our psychic experience we access the collective unconscious through archetypes, symbolic behavior, and ritual – predominantly through dreams, intuition, and imagination. (More in Jung's *Collected Works*, Vol.9).

Wisdom and Consciousness

In my review of the information explosion in Part Two above, I suggested that beyond the acquisition of information and knowledge is the challenge of utilizing *wisdom*, to grasp the deeper significance of what is transpiring in our rapidly changing world. I can now elaborate further on what that wisdom might look like. The Jewish scientist, Gerald Schroeder (2001, xi) offers this explanation:

> The discoveries of science, those that explore the molecular complexity of biology, and those who probe the brain/mind interface, have moved us to the brink of a startling realization: all existence is the expression of an all-encompassing wisdom that pervades the universe. Every particle, every being,

from atom to human, appears to have within it a level of information, of conscious wisdom. The information just appears as given, with no causal agent, as if it were an intrinsic facet of nature.

The search for meaning deep within has reshaped our spiritual sensibilities over recent decades, and concomitantly science encounters a deep sense of the sacred with increasing frequency. Psychological insight contributes to the same pursuit, moving significantly from the behaviorist perspective to the transpersonal and archetypal realms of human experience. Put all three strands together and we gain valuable insights into the modern fascination with consciousness. Out of the depths new wisdom arises!

For some commentators the evidence for this shift in consciousness can be seen in a renewed interest in meditation and the spiritual exploration of interiority –the pursuit of inner meaning. In the 1960s it veered significantly towards the East, adopting a range of meditation practices, with guru-like figures such as the Dalai Lama and Thích Nhất Hạnh attracting huge attention. There is another aspect to this awakening that has received only scant scholarly attention, and is likely to be a major multi-disciplinary development throughout the twenty-first century, namely, *the sacred nature of creation itself.*

A growing interest in the spirituality of indigenous peoples substantiates this connection: the land is the primary sacred reality, and the appropriation of that grounded sense of sanctity begets a quality of awareness congruent with the consciousness being described in this book. So, the shift in consciousness –the new embracing wisdom of our time –arises not from sophisticated metaphysical theories, religious or scientific, nor from those who flee the sinful world seeking the peace and tranquility of monastery or ashram. To the contrary, I suspect the consciousness is arising from the living earth itself, as it cries out for liberation from human despoliation.

Our indigenous peoples have known this earth-centered consciousness for thousands of years, a type of earthy mysticism our ancient ancestors would have known for several previous millennia, ritually depicted in the caves and rock-faces of Paleolithic times (cf. Lewis-Williams 2002). In humans today, that consciousness has morphed into the complexities of our self-reflexive endowments (our capacity to think about the fact that we can think). Tragically though, our psyches have become disconnected from the organic planetary web, and that is why we get it so desperately wrong in how we view the world and try to relate to it.

For far too long we, humans have dominated the landscape of creation. We deem ourselves to be the superior species, with special privilege under God (until we made Gods of ourselves), to lord it over everything else in the created world, and use the earth's resources for our own benefit and progress. This readily led to the dualistic split between the alive *human*, and the lifeless creation, which includes in between them other life-creatures such as, animals and plants. However, these life-creatures were always viewed as closer to the inanimate rather than the animate.

Our anthropocentric desire to reduce life to an observable, quantifiable source has never been achieved. Something illusive persistently haunts this pursuit. The consciousness falls short of our aspirations, or rather it is incapable of lifting our psychic wisdom to a level whereby the desires of the human heart are congruent with that which the living earth desires for us –and for all the other creatures with whom we share the planetary web of life. Embedded in this vision is the indigenous belief in the Great Spirit.

Not to be understood in religious terms, and certainly not an anthropocentric projection, the Great Spirit is generally understood to be a transpersonal, transformative force propelling evolution in its creative trajectory. It embodies all the key words I have used above: creativity, energy, spirituality and consciousness. And as indigenous peoples reclaim this enduring sense of Spirit power (explored at length in O'Murchu 2012), our search for the meaning of consciousness is likely to become more engaging and empowering.

Seeking Enlightenment

Several challenges ensue from these reflections, but let's stay with the lure highlighted in the last section. Despite the mental distractions that come our way each day, and all the false indoctrinations, highlighted in Part One, a range of spiritual awakenings characterizes our time. Not merely the mind, but our inner psyche wants to venture to new depths. Intuition, imagination and inspiration quicken our vitality. Critical awareness is on the increase, and an expansive global awareness is evident, particularly among the wise elders of our time (cf. Roszak 2009).

We need to trust this lure and follow where it leads. While we must not abandon rational wisdom, we need to recognize that linear thought patterns are not conducive to the evolutionary awakening we experience. The lateral mind, with its broad scope and soulful perception, is much more useful. Contrary to the spiritual wisdom of previous times, we embrace our cosmic and earthy groundedness, as we strive to belong beautifully to the clay from which we're formed.

Petrified clerics, and rabid fundamentalists, will shower us with scare tactics. Dogmatic denunciations will emerge from fear-filled entrenched institutions. All the forces on earth cannot halt the new rise in consciousness; that is a fidelity none of us can afford to compromise. Assuredly, the human mind can succumb to delusion –and that is as true of the guardians of orthodoxy as of the rest of us. In fact, there is growing evidence to show that the new consciousness springs anew from the ground up, and not from the top down. This is the paradigm shift popularized in scientific research of recent decades.

We need to trust the awakening, and flow with its momentum. It is a risky endeavor for which we will need the supportive vigilance of discerning soul-mates. There are no experts, but the consciousness itself initiates a sense of befriending and dialogue. In that shared wisdom, the risk becomes an adventure, and the endeavor paves the way to a new sense of enlightenment.

23. *The Wisdom to Embrace Paradox*

Be Alert to the LURE *of a universe thriving through paradox, throwing our neat dualistic categories into cultural disarray.*

What happened on the day after Christmas in 2004 was necessary for life. That may be hard to hear, but the kind of earthquake that created the tsunami is, literally, something the earth needs to do so that there is life. That earthquake was the result of one tectonic plate slipping underneath another. It is a form of recycling . ... This recycling makes the planet habitable. If the earth doesn't do this, life as we know it dies.

Margaret Swedish.

The people living along the coastal region of eastern Japan will never forget the tsunami of March 2011. With little warning and ferocious drive those waters tore through waterway and landmass, killing organic life (including humans), lifting vehicles, and carrying whole dwellings in its swell. The ensuing heaps of rubble and debris could only be described as images of hell on earth.

We are often told that life has an insurmountable resilience; and if millions believe in an omnipotent God, then how do we make any sense at all of such mindless and reckless destruction? And with increasing capricious activity in the natural realm in recent times – earthquakes, tornadoes, hurricanes, tsunamis – how do we face the future with some sense of confidence, and a reassurance for our own protection and safety?

I am sometimes accused of reckless utopianism, highlighting breakthroughs, while ignoring or bypassing the nasty stuff that creates such wanton pain and suffering in our world. So, let's honor the entire picture: chaos and creativity alike. And more daunting still, let's face the bewildering dilemma that the quantum lure of the future will also include cataclysmic forces that defy all sense of rationality and purpose.

The Great Paradox

We are dealing with paradox written large, a phenomenon I have elsewhere described (O'Murchu 2003; 2010; Swimme & Berry 1992) and will briefly review in the present work. There is a quantity and quality of destruction inherent to evolution at every time and in every cultural context. The destruction is inherent to the evolution of universal life. It is not an aberration, nor should it be rationalized as a fundamental flaw, which is a notion adopted by Christianity and by some other religions. *There is no flaw in the cosmic or planetary creation.* Instead, there is an abundance of *paradox*, much of which is quite baffling. There is a huge difference between a flawed situation and one characterized by paradox.

A useful example is that of earthquakes. In scientific terms an earthquake means a shifting in the earth's tectonic plates, which among other things involves a clearing away of surplus wastage, and thus facilitates the earth-body to function in a healthier way. If we had no earthquakes, we would not have the viable planet we have today, with its vast array of life forms and living systems. Earthquakes are essential – absolutely crucial – to the viability of planet Earth.

The religious believer will ask: Is this how God created the world? Did the same God also create the paradoxes that characterize our creation? The religionist wants to hear a negative response, but that would be inauthentic. The creative life force – divine or otherwise – is also the source and sustenance of the destruction. Through and through – at every level from that of the macroscopic universe to the microscopic bacterium - the same evolutionary process is observable: creation is endowed with *the paradox of creation-and-destruction*, otherwise named as a process of birth-death-rebirth. It cannot be otherwise. The paradox is the foundation for freedom and creativity. Get rid of the paradox and all we have left is total nihilism.

The art of befriending

At this time of major evolutionary transition, we are likely to encounter an increase in paradoxical fallout. It is already apparent in the turbulence that characterizes the earth and its life-systems. More erratic and unpredictable weather patterns, intense and heavily destructive storms, natural disasters and cataclysmic events are likely to characterize our future. And we will need a very different understanding of faith to make sense of what will be transpiring.

We cannot get rid of the paradoxical element in creation, but more baffling still, we cannot control it according to the criteria of patriarchal management. We cannot suppress earthquake activity, but we can learn to befriend the earthquake, thus enabling us to contain its destructive impact. In the United States and Canada, in Japan and Malaysia, and in several other parts of the world, we have erected earthquake resistant buildings, thus minimizing the loss of human life when an earthquake occurs.

Some very serious concerns arise at this juncture, particularly related to justice and a more equitable distribution of human resources. In 2005, an earthquake registering 7.4 on the Richter scale, hit Pakistan, with ensuing human casualties of 240,000 people. Why did God inflict this calamity, the people queried. "Was God trying to punish us for some infidelity?" they asked. These were the questions raised by many of the predominantly Muslim population. It is not God's problem and as long as we keep invoking God, we will be searching in vain for an authentic explanation. It is a human problem not a divine one.

We know how to resolve it in the rich nations, with the wealth, technology, and engineering to create earthquake resistant buildings. When an earthquake of great magnitude - 8.00 on the Richter scale - erupted in the island of Guam in 1991, there were no human casualties, despite significant structural damage; the island is an American colony and all the buildings are earthquake-resistant. We could have done the same in Pakistan had we the sense of justice and equality to share the human resources, so readily available in the richer nations.

Who is responsible for the death of the 240,000 people in Pakistan? *The human family at large is responsible.* More specifically our imperial world governments have to shoulder this grave responsibility. Foundationally, the problem is one of ignorance: we do not understand how creation's paradox works, and one is left with the impression that many of our powerful leaders (and their selective elites) would prefer not to know. Millions don't even know about the paradox, so how can we hope to engage with it in a more responsive and responsible way?

Those who do know are those who have learned to befriend the consciousness I described in the last section. And often these are not the elite of our academic institutions, nor the mighty of the earth, but those we frequently dismiss as primitive and uncivilized. Like the Morgan fisher folks of South Western Thailand, who on December 26, 2004, read intelligently nature's signals of the impending tsunami, moved up into the hills and suffered no casualties. Indeed, the wise shall inherit the earth. Many of our indigenous peoples know how to befriend paradox, but we would rather denounce their primitive instinct, instead of adopting their archetypal wisdom.

Whither the Power of the Cross?

The problem is even more subtle –and sinister –in a religion like Christianity. We misname the paradox as a flaw, and seek an external divine rescuer to resolve the dilemma for us. We posit a divine savior who himself embraces the paradox through his death on a Cross. We conceptualize the person of Jesus as a paradigmatic scapegoat, who does all the dirty work on our behalf. Now, we can wait for the redemption, which he has wrought on our behalf. This must be one of the greatest cop-outs of all time, one that has exacerbated further the cruel suffering of millions of people, not to mention the suffering earth itself and its many other exploited life forms.

God, for those who hold such a belief, *is in the paradox*, not above it, nor outside it. The death of Jesus is emblematic of the price paid for a life of radical engagement with the prevailing paradoxes of the time. In a word, Jesus was killed because of the bold, prophetic way he lived. Christian salvation (redemption) is in the paradigmatic life of Jesus, as a prophetic befriender of the oppressed and marginalized, and not in the ignominious death he endured at the hands of those who could no longer tolerate his creative empowerment of the masses at the margins. Redemptive death is not the solution. Bold prophetic befriending is the authentic way forward.

A rescuing God paralyses creativity, human and divine. Christian faith, and the core truth of all the great religions, is based on an empowering vision described in the Christian Gospels as the *Kingdom of God.* In the original Aramaic language of the historical Jesus it may be translated as the *Companionship of Empowerment* (more in O'Murchu 2011). The life of Jesus is paradigmatic, not a stereotypical sacrificial victim – a favored construct of all patriarchal religion – but as a prophetic catalyst, who liberates a new sense of how humans can engage with life's challenges including the chaotic paradoxes upon which creation flourishes.

To engage the paradoxes, we need to be both robust and humble: "wise as serpents and clever as doves." Christian faith, which embraces the *Companionship of Empowerment,* calls forth a quality of adulthood, which many religions have grossly neglected. This is the robust faith that will lure us with greater hope and promise into the evolutionary complexities of the twenty-first century. Thus the wisdom we need to sustain us is one that can embrace paradox — befriending it intelligently, and addressing its challenge through a more concerted effort to reconstruct a world-order characterized by a more just and equitable distribution of the resources with which our earth is blessed abundantly.

Paradox is here to stay, and as the lure of evolution gathers more momentum in the 21st century, we are likely to encounter more baffling and destructive paradoxes. There is no point in waiting on God to resolve this dilemma for us. We have been blessed with the personal wisdom, and the resourceful creation, to engage more creatively and responsibly with these enormous challenges. This is a collaborative challenge, requiring whole new ways of working and cooperating together – the subject to which we turn attention in the next section.

$$\approx \diamond \approx$$

24. *The Relational Adult: Autopoiesis & Human Cooperation*

Be Alert to the Lure of a new wave of eroticism with a divine precedent that changes even the atomistic foundations of science itself.

I become who I will be within the network of relations, rooted in the non-human, blooming in the intimate, branching into the unknown.

Catherine Keller.

The Spirit of Ubuntu –that profound African sense that we are human only through the humanity of other human beings –is not a parochial phenomenon, but has added globally to our common search for a better world.

Nelson Mandela.

The survival of the fittest is a powerful ideology, deeply ingrained in the human psyche. Long before Charles Darwin carved his renowned theory of evolution –with nuances that many neo-Darwinians fail to acknowledge –the survival instinct was uppermost in human consciousness. Life is a battle, we have so often been told. Thus the harder you fight the better your chances of survival. Such a battle requires intelligence, but far more important, it requires muscle, nerve and a daring disposition.

Survival is something you prove by the power of your might. The focus is strongly externalized. The competitive leverage belongs to success in business, above all in making money. And the more opponents you can eliminate on the way, the better your changes of flourishing.

Educationally, this translates into success in examinations, in sports, in all school activities. External barometers determine how successful the pupil has been and how he/she is likely to excel in the open playing field of daily life. After schooling you move on to proving your worth as a competent adult, and that is measured by the following attainments: *independence, family* and *work*. In practice this tripartite focus translates into: *a job, heterosexual marriage, a mortgage, life insurance, children, the family car, retirement plans, making a will.*

The Human Agent

These expectations translate into three aspects of our social functioning, which essentially determine whether a person is considered useful or not:

a) Civic responsibility exercised mainly through employment – holding down a regular job.

b) Domestic responsibility exercised through monogamous, heterosexual marriage, which normally required creating one's own home.

c) Cultural responsibility exercised through

procreation of new life and the furtherance of the patriarchal culture through the institution of the family.

Millions still assume these criteria to be normative and essential for the social, political and economic functioning of society. Millions judge their personal worth and value by these standards, and assess the authenticity of others by how well they measure up in achieving these targets. The human person is perceived to be a *functional* agent, enhancing the performance of a *mechanistic* global system. The human is a component in the wheel of progress, an atomistic functionary bouncing around like the proverbial billiard balls — all deemed necessary to make up the scientific whole, but each functioning primarily on the basis of its individualistic resourcefulness. It is a world of lone rangers, quite alien to the relational web of life.

Human agency is a favored concept in philosophy and a time-honored category in the literature of the social sciences. It denotes the useful citizen: as propagator, manufacturer, moneymaker and institutional stalwart. Since males fulfill these expectations in a more obvious way, they become the primary models of authentic humanity. Despite significant changes in the late twentieth century, men are still paid higher wages, hold down more leadership roles, have legal and religious privileges denied to women, and are widely admired for greater strength and wisdom. On closer examination, the notion of human agency is a corrupt and deviant distortion.

Much more disturbing is the widespread patriarchal inculturation with worldwide reinforcement. In every modern educational system we adopt the understanding of the human person Aristotle bequeathed to us. Authentic humanness is characterized by *autonomy, independence, separateness, rationality*; the true human stands over and above every other organism in creation. This is the imperial self, the inflated ego, unknown to humans for most of our seven-million-year evolutionary history, but perpetuated in our time by education, politics, social policy and religion. It is a kind of cultural dogma that nobody dares to question, and very few do. It is one of the most serious distortions confronting our species today.

Towards the Relational Self

The nature of human agency will need to change drastically. If it doesn't, then we are in all likelihood, taking a major step in the direction of our own self-destruction. Our manipulation of the earth and its resources has reached a level of being non-sustainable, either for the earth itself or for the creatures inhabiting our planet, including our own species. Because our interference has been so compulsively driven, it is doubly difficult for us to disengage meaningfully.

So, where will that leave humanity? Were we not commanded to till the earth and subdue it? And have we not reaped enormous benefit by doing so? Indeed, all the major religions to one degree or another have sanctioned gross human interference simply because patriarchal religion as we know it today evolved initially in the wake of the Agricultural Revolution (a fact that is generally not acknowledged). And the benefits we have reaped have been largely to the advantage of humans, but not so for several other creatures nor for the living earth itself.

The problem in our time is that such unsustainable behavior has become so normalized. We no longer can discern what enhances genuine human-ness and what militates against it. For so long we have internalized the archetypal lone-ranger, depicted in ancient times in the fierce hunter, the meat-eater, the conqueror, the survivor, and the warrior seeking to win in all the great battles of life.

A very different image of the human has been emerging in the anthropology and psychology of recent decades, with quite a radical re-evaluation of what constitutes the inner life of human nature. In the opening decade of the twenty-first century we evidenced the publication of such scholarly works as Jeremy Rifkin's *The Empathic Civilization* (Rifkin 2009), Franz de Waal's *The Age of Empathy* (de Waal 2010), and *The Compassionate Instinct* (Dacher Keltner & Alia 2010). Nobody can refute the serious scientific basis of these works. Not merely do they forthrightly challenge long-standing views to the contrary, but they highlight the corrupt imperial worldview we humans have espoused for far too long.

In our deep inner selves we are programmed for cooperation, not for competition, for mutuality and relationship, not for functional agency. I am at all times the sum of my relationships; that's what constitutes my deepest, God-given identity. In my deep inner being, I am programmed to relate, not to compete.

As human persons, our essential identity is molded out of a vast web of relationships, embracing our parents, siblings, peers, friends and work-colleagues. But that relational web also includes the other life forms with which I share planet Earth, along with the living earth itself and the cosmos to which all life belongs. In the formative influences of my natal development several scientific fields interweave and inform the reproductive process. Each human body represents a rich interface of cosmic, planetary, social and personal influences. Each human life is a tapestry of stories, relational narratives that span billions of years of creative evolution.

The Genial Gene

The notion of *the selfish gene*, popularized by the biologist, Richard Dawkins, posited a linear mechanical direction to all living systems, congruent with the neo-Darwinian notion of the survival of the fittest. Dawkins claims that genes govern and control all behavior with one goal always to the fore: self-perpetuation. Many biologists support this view, one that is quite at variance with a less popular set of insights, but no less ingenious, that came to be known as the science of *epigenetics*.

The newly developing field of epigenetics claims that genes do not control our life. Our perceptions, emotions, beliefs, and attitudes actually rewrite our genetic code (more in Lipton 2005). Through our perceptions, we can modify every gene in our body, and create thirty thousand variations from every gene just by the way we respond to life. In short, we are leaving behind a reality of victimization (by our genes) and moving into the awareness that our mind – our consciousness, the immaterial realm – influences our experience and creative potential. We are co-participants in the organizing wisdom of our embodied selves, when we choose to honor a wisdom greater than our rational minds, yet inherent to our evolutionary well-being – hence the provocative notion of *the genial gene*, developed by the biologist Joan Roughgarden (2009).

The Human Genome Project was supposed to verify the model that genes create life and to show us the more than 150,000 genes that are involved, but the project finished with only 23,000 genes, indicating that several aspects of human behavior arise from other influences. So, if genes are not the final arbiters, determining behaviour (which is Dawkin's notion of the selfish gene), then what role do they actually play, and what/who now occupies the higher ground? Relationality becomes the focus of attention, as energy flows through the cell membrane interacting relationally under several influences of the surrounding environment. The medical scientist, Bruce Lipton (2005) and educationalist, Dawson Church (2007) make these newly empowering insights comprehensible to the general public.

The Relational Landscape

Quantum physics imagines relationality as the ambience within which everything in creation grows and flourishes. The new cosmology redefines interconnectedness – and not adversarial atomism – as the core stuff of the universe. Throughout the closing decades of the twentieth century, theorists from a range of disciplines highlighted the central role of nature's inherent capacity for self-organization, scientifically named as *autopoiesis*. Originally introduced by Chilean biologists, Humberto Maturana and Francisco Varela in 1972, the concept highlights an internal symbiosis in living systems which cannot be explained in terms of cause-and-effect. Several commentators equate *autopoiesis* with the notion of self-organization (Jantsch 1980; Kaufmann 1993), although Maturana and Varela did not support that equivalence.

Mary Midgley (2010, 105) describes self-organization as the mysterious generation of patterns from within. Living systems are characterized by something akin to an internalized wisdom (consciousness), which enables the system to move in the direction of growth, development and complexity. It is an interactive process, mobilized by evolution's preference for interconnectedness above and beyond our favored theories of adversarial conflict.

The late Lynn Margulis (1998) highlighted the same relational orientation in the behavior of primordial bacteria, the organic basis of all life forms. From the bacteria, to humanity, to the earth, and the enveloping cosmos, relationality is the default position, and relationship is the vital link through which everything grows and flourishes. Humans therefore must reconsider our mechanistic regard for the living earth and our inherited tendency to subdivide it into functional units. That quality of engagement is no longer sustainable at any level. We must revision another way of being planetary earthlings, the challenge taken up in our next Section.

25. *Bioregional Empowerment*

Be Alert to the Lure of the earth-body yearning for a restructuring that will reclaim and honor its organic creativity.

Order and design are values too, but if nature were perfectly designed, it could never give rise to the drama of life.

John F. Haught

If humans want to move into a more collaborative, cooperative way of living –which I suspect is the direction in which evolution is pushing us –then we will also have to evaluate and reform a number of institutional structures we have heretofore taken so much for granted. Foremost is the notion of the nation state itself.

Of all the obstacles facing humanity in the evolutionary call to co-create a better future, the nation state is probably the single greatest barrier. The adoption of the state as the primary instrument for government came to the fore in the eighteenth century, and flourishes on the ideology of the divine right of kings. It also thrives on the basis of warfare, the strategy used in the evolution of most nation states in the modern world.

The doomed Nation State

As indicated in Part One, the nation state is a highly problematic institution, and has proved deeply unsatisfactory in terms of mobilizing human ingenuity and creativity. It has flourished on the basis of the will-to-power, reinforced by a small powerful cohort of largely dominant males. Had it not the support and validation of religion it would have floundered long ago.

In recent decades, the nation state has given way to the transnational corporation (TNC). The wealth and resourcefulness of the state is now largely in the hands of corporations. Corporations control the flow of money; they dictate the value of goods (through patenting) and they monopolize commerce and trade around the world. Most deleterious of all, they shift work-outlets around the planet to take advantage of the cheapest labor force, thus leaving millions with an unpredictable and uncertain future. This is just one of several destructive tendencies over which national governments have little or no control.

Another limitation of the nation state is its anthropocentric bias. The state is interested first and foremost in the welfare of its citizens; it exists to serve the needs of people (allegedly). It colludes with the view that the material creation is there for the benefit of humankind, and concurs with the objectification and wanton destruction of nature. Ironically, it is precisely because of this distorted perception that several nations backed the establishment and working strategy of the WTO, set up in 1994 to provide corporations with the ability to organize global trade and commerce.

The nation state sought to prioritize humans and their needs. In time, this translated into prioritizing the powerful and the rich, thus betraying the desires of most of humanity. But the betrayal was much more devious, because by prioritizing the human over and above the natural world, the state was undermining the organic web of life without which people cannot live with value and dignity. In a sense the state has always been a doomed institution promoting a doomed vision for humanity and the world.

Beyond the Nation State

In a landmark book, Anne Wilson Schaef (1988) pronounces a piercing critique of all patriarchal institutions including the nation state, as institutions in the grip of an unrelenting addiction that will not easily be broken. As the philosophy (spirituality) of Alcoholics Anonymous highlights, addictions can only be surrendered, rarely (if ever) consciously changed. In other words, in the depth of anguish or despair we let go of addiction in a kind of mystical abandonment, an indefinable trust that something better will emerge to replace the dysfunctional behavior we have known and loved. How to apply this resolution to major institutions – social and political – is a much more onerous undertaking.

As a substitute for the nation state, we know of alternatives that are much more likely to produce more benign and empowering outcomes. Of particular significance is the notion of the bioregion. The roots of *bioregionalism* go back to the 1930s when Fredric Clements and Victor Shelford developed the biome system of classification. Biomes refer to natural habitats such as grasslands, deserts, rainforests and coniferous forests shaped by climate. Particular soils, vegetation and animal life developed in each climate-region in accordance with rainfall, temperature and weather patterns.

The *bioregion* may be described as both a geographical terrain and a realm of consciousness. It is a new and different way of conceptualizing the human relationship with the earth and its resources. Significantly, it begins with the organic giftedness of the earth itself, and invites humans to work within that inherited framework – almost the complete opposite of the philosophy of nationalism.

Kirkpatrick Sale (1991: 50ff) identifies four central features of bioregional engagement:

> a) Global socio-economic abstractions give way to the here and now, to what is seen and felt, to the real and the known. The human body is grounded in the earth-body. The emerging sense of self is more rooted and organic.
>
> b) The cycle of production and exchange is determined primarily by the quality and quantity of local resources. People become much more aware of the creative cycle of life, and of the need to participate responsibly – and sustainably – in how we appropriate the resources of the earth.
>
> c) A very different kind of political civility comes to the fore. Mutual co-responsibility is likely to become the central strategy. People begin to realize that the earth itself is an empowering life-source, which deserves a congruent affirmation from humans who also need to develop strategies of empowerment that will impact positively upon the earth itself as well as upon human beings. d)New interdependent strategies are likely to evolve: families operating within neighborhoods, neighborhoods within communities,

communities within cities, etc. Cooperation rather than competition becomes a core value. This is a polity already familiar to humans through our indigenous peoples around the world.

Bioregionalism is far more integral to the biotic structure of the earth's ecosystem(s). It also provides a grounding much more likely to satisfy and fulfill the authentic needs of humans themselves. By maintaining our gaze on those values through which the earth itself flourishes, human beings also thrive, and have their needs met in a deeper and more integrated way. How this happens is spelt out by Thomas Berry (1985) in his list of primary bioregional (ecological) values: *self-emergence, self-nourishing, self-propagating, self-educating, self-healing, self-governing, and self-fulfilling.* By attending to the living earth as an organic self, with needs and developmental potential, we automatically enhance our own need and potential for growth, advancement and the attainment of our deeper potentials.

From the real to the ideal!

An option for bioregionalism as a new political strategy for the future is inconceivable at the present time. Too many people live in ignorance, and the prevailing powers in our time are determined to maintain the status quo of power and domination. Once again we encounter an impasse which on the one hand we know to be real, but we also suspect that it is much more fragile than the guardians of orthodoxy realize. That being the case, it is absolutely right that we explore alternatives. We may need to adopt them sooner than most of us realize.

The critics of globalization have, for some time now, been pointing us to a healthier and more empowering alternative, namely *localization* (Hines 2000). The emphasis is on the need to develop and support local markets, so that people have a more direct and empowering sense of participation in their own wellbeing, as distinct from the anonymity and homogenization imposed by transnational corporations who have little or no interest in local empowerment unless it benefits them financially. As used in this context, localization refers to a socially empowering local form of resourcing, and not merely a translation business supplementing globalization as envisaged in the 1980s.

Our dysfunctional empire building cannot continue indefinitely. Too many people are alienated, and the suffering earth itself is not likely to tolerate the abuse indefinitely. We are already witnessing a political and economic counter-culture, which will become more visible and enduring when the consciousness is there to support it. Several examples of bioregional initiative have been studied and proposed (Douthwaite 1998, Hines 2000; Suzuki 2002; Greco 2009). Some have worked well, but have not received the media attention they deserve. Just as governments around the world have sought to suppress or co-opt NGOs (non-governmental organizations), so too with bioregionalism. The climate as yet is too hostile to its adoption and flourishing. But there is good reason to believe that it will have its day – and if we wish to be participants in that breakthrough it is wise to inform ourselves of the potential that lies in the future.

26. *Earthing our Way to Non-violence*

Be Alert for the Lure of the broken-hearted, sick of warfare and violence, and crying out for a nonviolent engagement with life at every level.

We humans are not slaughter-prone assassins by nature.

Donna Hart & Robert Sussman.

I am not going to quote the sickening statistics –they are available on several web pages. We know that the twentieth century was the bloodiest in human history. And the twenty-first century began with a series of wars – Iraq, Afghanistan, Sri Lanka, the Congo, Sudan, and many more – resulting in the hidden casualties of several million innocent women, men and children. We hear and see the violent plight of military personnel, but rarely the cruel toll on innocent civilians (predominantly women and children) with the home planet itself polluted and defaced by the stench of warfare.

Thanks to popular media we are exposed on a daily basis to the horrors of modern conflicts. We could easily assume that most of humanity spends most of its time and money fighting over something or other. Paradoxically, it is a false and misleading distortion. Most people live amicably and peacefully. Cooperation rather than competition rules the roost. Millions of people every day negotiate contracts, agreements, business deals, using human dialogue, negotiating skill and non-violent persuasion. It does not hit headlines. It is not sensational. Yet, it is the stuff that makes the world go-round, and without this altruistic capacity, humanity would have become extinct millions of years ago.

Humanity under review

Because of the various distortions outlined in Part One, humans today inhabit a perceptual dark hole of our own making, one that we, and we alone, can change and reconstruct. It has nothing to do with some fundamental flaw, called original sin, or by any other name. Underlying most of the distortions in Part One is an option for violence. It is endemic to the patriarchal way of being, of seeing, and of acting. And it evolved primarily in the wake of the Agricultural Revolution, some 8,000-10,000 years ago, when a leading aggressive sub-group, consisting mainly of dominant males who initiated a new regime of patriarchal power. This new emergence set humans over against the living earth itself. They began to commodify the material creation, divide it up into manageable sections, and parcel it out in units, which several thousand years later would morph into nation states.

Large-scale warfare is inextricably linked to nation states. Its precursor can be traced to the shadow side of the agricultural revolution, dating back perhaps 8,000 years, when we first started dividing up the planet in an artificial and capricious way. Rival groups began to fight over land, which progressively was commodified and sanctioned under the patriarchal God into the "divine" institutions that we know today. Even the visionary dream of the United Nations has been usurped and seriously undermined by the ideology of the nation state.

Throughout the twentieth century, studies in paleontology and anthropology have challenged and altered several cultural assumptions that prevailed in earlier times, including the rather confused notion of the noble savage popularized by both Thomas Hobbes and Jean-Jacques Rousseau. A benign and more wholesome view has been invoke, thanks to a more thorough research on several tribal cultures. One key insight still remains to be verified and established. It is this: *when humans remain very close to nature, as we seem to have done for millions of years in our long evolutionary story, then for the greater part we behave in a convivial and non-violent manner*. We did remain close to nature for most of the time; consequently, we got it right for most of our evolutionary pathway. If that is the underlying core of our human nature – the primary driving force of our cultural and human *raison d'etre* - then we have the innate potential to become more authentically human again, as a non-violent, creative species.

I know it sounds incredulous to modern sensibilities. It even sounds bizarre! The stop valve of civilization continues to hinder us from looking too deeply into our ancient past. The barrier of religion is still firmly established between the primitive and the sacred, despite the fact that several other fields of study have removed that barrier throughout the course of the twentieth century. The progress of that century ridicules those who suggest that we have much to learn from our deep past. And for the moneymakers – economists and advertisers – it is too much of a distraction from the fierce competition so desperately needed to keep the modern world spinning around.

Spinning around, or spinning out of control? Every developed nation spends millions, and some even billions, each year to keep violence and destruction at bay. The United States alone has enough nuclear weapons to destroy not just one, but ten planets of our size. On closer examination we cannot dodge the conclusion that it is our cultural and political investment in violent weaponry that is feeding the culture of violence itself. Violence begets violence, and contributes virtually nothing to the more peaceful world millions of people yearn for.

Our non-violent future

Is a non-violent future possible? If we achieved it in former times, why can't we do so again? In one sense this might well be the biggest quantum leap facing humanity today. And if we fail to make the transition to a non-violent way of living, I don't think there is the slightest doubt of what will transpire: we will annihilate ourselves – we will indeed enter recorded history as the sixth major extinction!

A non-violent world is possible, and it does not take a rare genius to figure out some of the steps that would lead us in that direction:

   a) A new way of perceiving

   b) A new way of retrieving

   c) A new way of relating

   d) A new way of political restructuring

Seeing in Context

In the 1980s, the biologist, Rupert Sheldrake, developed the notion of *morphic resonance*, popularly known as the one-hundredth-monkey syndrome. The theory indicates that one does not need massive numbers to bring about a movement for the better (a paradigm shift). What is needed more than anything else is a strong coherence among the subgroup making the shift to a new way of being, which always begins with a new way of seeing (More in Sheldrake 2009). In our age of mass information, we possess many of the elements of being able to see differently. Unfortunately, the information is usurped and manipulated by a handful of media tycoons who twist and distort the contents to sensationalize power. Sadly most people have not been educated to detect and transcend the ensuing superficiality.

Our hope for the future rests in the fact that more and more people are becoming suspicious, and are venturing to voice their skepticism and dissent. Lets not forget the old scholastic dictum: *action follows thought*. When enough people begin to think differently, when our perpetual morphic resonance moves to greater coherence and conviction, then even the violent empire that so dominates our world begins to lose its monopoly. Evolution will be on the side of those who choose the way of non-violence.

Retrieving the Noble Savage

It strikes me that we humans were never noble savages. It is a myth we need to abandon. We were historic earthlings absorbed in nature, with an instinctual intuitive interconnectedness we have long lost in the excessively rational culture of civilized times. As already indicated it is this disconnection from the living earth, and our consequent confiscation of the earth-body as a financial commodity, that has led to the violence that now threatens to overwhelm us.

I am not recommending a regression to some idyllic past. Evolution never moves backward. The challenge facing us is one of retrieval, reconnecting with an ancient wisdom and reclaiming a more earth-centered spirituality. We have violated our foundational organic nature. We live in a violent, unsustainable relationship with the living web that has birthed us. We need to learn a new way of connecting and inter-relating. A more discerning appropriation of our deep past will empower us to move forward in a more enlightened and authentic way.

Cooperation rather than competition

In a previous Section, I highlighted recent scholarly research substantiating our innate drive for cooperation and not for fierce competition. Not merely does warfare and violence destroy our human and earthly lives, our appropriation of conflict and adversarial bargaining is alien to our fundamental nature. As creatures programmed for mutual empowerment, we undermine the very essence of our humanity in the violent behavior that has become endemic to our civilization.

We associate the notion of healing with infirmity of body and mind, with sickness and bodily suffering. But in fact what we need first and foremost is *systemic healing* and not resources merely for greater human wholeness. The institutional structures we have adopted – political, social, and financial – are all conflict-ridden and violently dysfunctional. In particular, our attitude to land as a commodity over which we fight and die is distinctly bizarre. As a species we have lost all sense of the integral and organic nature of the web of life to which we belong.

Healing, therefore, will employ a shift in our awareness, and an openness to reconciliation, not with the adversary, but with our own deluded selves. Forgiveness is a concept for which there is little room in our strive-ridden lifestyles. We are indoctrinated into more fighting and struggling to get things right. Even our legal system – intended to enhance right relating - has been absorbed into the violent merry-go-round. Unfortunately, it is often employed to justify might over right.

The beginnings of a new model of jurisprudence, namely *Restorative Justice* (web page: http://en.wikipedia.org/wiki/ Restorative_justice) is much more conducive to a culture of non-violence. It incorporates all the elements outlined above: a different awareness, healing, reconciliation, and forgiveness. It requires mutual engagement of offender and offended, and where possible, all in the wider community affected by the destructive (criminal) behavior, in an attempt to restore right relationships for the empowerment of all involved. Thus far we have some promising and encouraging experiments from both New Zealand and Canada.

No more land to fight for

Bioregional reorganization is postulated on the fact that the land is a living organism for the engagement and participation of humans more enlightened and aware of their own true nature. Non-violence is not merely about abandoning violent ways of behaving. Rather it involves a radical shift in understanding, espousing all the new insights explored in this book.

The land is the foundational biotic community, the primary example of interdependent, cooperative living, embracing within that larger view, the paradox of birth-death-rebirth reviewed in Section 23 above. Non-violent adaptation requires of humans the adjustment to move away from our imperial domination and become a servant species to the empowering vitality of the living earth itself. It sounds like an enterprise almost impossible to envisage, never mind, embrace. Such is the extent of our addiction to the currently violent way of living.

It will not be an easy conversion, but already by the end of the twenty-first century, in all probability, the precarious plight of Homo sapiens will leave us with little other option than to make the inconceivable choice. The evolutionary lure will have once more caught up with humanity. We will follow where evolution will lead, a painfully turbulent transition for humans and a non-violent breakthrough for the living earth itself.

≈ ◇ ≈

27. *Sustainable Economics*

Be alert to the Lure of the corruption of Capitalism, and the yearning for new models of sustainability and gifting congruent with the living earth itself.

I propose that money arose as a means of facilitating gift-giving, sharing, and generosity, or at least that it bore something of that spirit. To recreate a sacred economy, it is necessary to restore to money that original spirit.

Charles Eisenstein

As indicated in Part One, our current capitalistic economic system seems to be in deep trouble, and there is no shortage of critical analyses varying from those claiming that capitalism is a spent force that should be abandoned, to the majority seeking to repair the system and make it more efficient. Whether we hold on to capitalism in some mitigated form, or opt for totally new financial alternatives, there is a wide convergence on what a more sustainable future looks like. That is the material I wish to review in the present section.

I am attempting to synthesize a vast plethora or overabundance of creative ideas that have evolved over the past thirty years, written up in books and journals, or available in more condensed form in a range of online web-pages.

Sustainability as an economic value

Thomas Greco (2009, 50) offers the following resume of our current financial impasse:

> Government and banking have colluded to create a political money system that embodies a "debt imperative" that results in a "growth imperative," which forces environmental destruction and rends the social fabric while increasing the concentration of

power and wealth. It creates economic and political instabilities that manifest in recurrent cycles of depression and inflation, domestic and international conflict, and social dislocation.

In this statement we encounter all the wrong moves, which immediately suggests what needs to be altered. Central to any improvement is the notion of a more sustainable economics. This means creating monetary systems and procedures whereby government and banks become more transparent and mutually accountable. The accountability in question is not merely to human beings. It will also need to involve how natural resources are used, valued, and traded.

Sustainability is quite a complex concept, and is often subverted in the functional approaches adopted by financial institutions and governments. As Bernard Lietaer (2002) indicates, money is first and foremost a form of energy; how we channel that energy, how we engage with it, and utilize it, cannot be reduced to a set of mechanistic procedures in which some control the energy-flow on behalf of others. Most people are not even aware of this basic fact. The big institutions have objectified money into a utilitarian commodity, and so have the masses. Both collude in the dysfunctional mess in which we find ourselves. Sustainability begins with awareness, and cannot be maintained without an extensive use of imagination. Every attempt at discerning what an alternative economics might look like emphasizes the need for participation and involvement in financial management. Money should belong first and foremost to people, and not to patriarchal financial institutions. Then, as in the barter system of earlier times, people become more aware of the value of money and the value of the goods for which exchanges are being negotiated. People do not think merely in terms of profit and greed; they think in terms of value and mutual enrichment.

The alternative vision goes much deeper, and has been lucidly formulated by Charles Eisenstien (2011) in his clarion call to reclaim the significance of money as a medium for gift-exchange. Above all else *money denotes giftedness*, people's desire to gift each other in the service of a deeper and more expansive mutuality. This quality of human regard – with its re-conceptualizing of money and its significance – is only possible when humans appreciate the giftedness of the living earth, and all it bestows for our growth and endowment. With this awareness, humans learn to reciprocate for all they have received. Gratitude becomes our default position. Another world can be called into being.

This is not a romantic ideal. For most of human history, humans created and managed their finances in a mutually enriching way. The bank of England only came into being in 1694, and the first bank in the United States was established in 1781. Banks initially were accountable to the people rather than to governments. The collusive control of the present time between banks and governments is very much an outcome of the twentieth century. Returning financial power to the people is a central responsibility for a more sustainable and effective economics for the future.

What do we mean by wealth?

In a seminal work in the early 1990s, Paul Elkins and Manfred Max-Neef co-edited an inspiring set of essays on the notion of wealth creation (Elkins & Max Neef 1992). Instead of reducing wealth to the accumulation of capital, or the extortion of finance to provide a veneer for being wealthy, the authors highlight a wider concept of wealth which money and financial systems are meant to serve and support.

Capital first and foremost belongs to the richness inherent in the living earth itself. We become rich or impoverished depending on how we engage with the capital that belongs to the web of life. In this expansive view, Elkins and Max-Neef explore five types of wealth (capital) that need to be embraced in a more comprehensive and empowering monetary system:

1. *Environmental Capital (EC)* expands beyond the idea of land to include all natural systems, such as the atmosphere, biological systems, and even the sun. Beyond the wealth of nations (and of peoples) is the richness inherent to the material cosmic creation itself, providing a vast repertoire of chemical and biological resources that define and empower the web of life. Sunlight is one of the more obvious examples, empowering the process of photosynthesis, which in turn nurtures all organic life that belongs to our home planet, the Earth.

2. *Human Capital (HC)* According to Elkins and Max-Neef, human capital has three components: health, knowledge and skills, and motivation. Human capital denotes the transpersonal endowments that empower humans to be agents for cultural transformation. Health, knowledge and motivation may be described as the internal capital, which enriches our own well-being and advancement, but also enables us to enhance the life-quality not merely of other humans but of all other creatures with whom we share the planetary web of life. 3.

Social and Organizational Capital (SOC) includes all of the interpersonal "software" that enables societies and organizations to function: habits, norms, roles, traditions, regulations, policies, etc. - in other words, the non-physical part of culture. SOC is different from HC in that HC is attached to a particular individual (you can walk out the door with it) while SOC provides the wherewithal to form a range of different relationships through which a culture of sharing and caring is established and maintained. Without this interactive context, we cannot honor our foundational human orientation for cooperation, and for the other suppressed potentials noted in earlier sections of this book.

4. *Manufactured Capital (MC)* includes, as in the conventional picture, buildings, tools, and equipment. Since Elkins and Max-Neef first outlined this expanded view, the industrial sphere has changed dramatically. It is now driven more by technology than by human effort, leading to massive under-employment and displacement of skilled labor. The recycling and disposal of waste has also become a much more problematic issue.

5. *Credit Capital* (CC) is specifically defined as a reservoir of credits and promises, so it includes money and debt, but not stocks or deeds, which are ownership rights tied to other forms of capital. In a more general sense, it includes all the strategies we use to accumulate wealth, along with the deluding self-perception that our true value is equivalent to the money we own and the material goods we possess.

CC leads to range of behaviors we largely take for granted, spread between earning money at one end of the spectrum and spending it at the other end. Our popular culture of consumption, driven by rabid advertising, rarely allows us to step back and review more critically and reflectively how money dominates our thinking, and drives our activity, at virtually every moment of our existence.

Our tendency to isolate and view money as a device for purchasing wealth and privilege is a systemic distortion that undermines the creative empowerment of money itself. As a form of energy, money belongs to the fabric of universal life (everything in creation is constituted by energy), and at all times needs to be used in conjunction with a creative and responsible use of all the earth's resources. Human relationships flourish when energy is congruent with energy; the same applies to a sustainable interface on how we use money to access the other goods of creation whether they are the natural phenomena of wind and water, mineral resources, or agricultural produce.

It follows, therefore, that governmental financial management and banks are meant to be service agencies facilitating the people in more congruent ways to exercise their monetary responsibilities. Similarly, such meaning also applies for international trade agencies. What have any of us to gain from aggressive corporations greedily appropriating goods for their own lucrative advancement while millions of people are starving and living in despicable poverty — with the living earth itself exploited, polluted and ravaged? It makes no sense whatever.

Parliamentarians know it makes no sense, but are now so enmeshed in the ideology of empire building that they no longer know how to care for the Earth community (see Korten 2006). Contrary to all the empty rhetoric, they do not have the people's best interests at heart. They often ply trade with popular consumerism, luring people into behaviors that are unsustainable in the short and long terms, and will eventually accrue in greater pain and suffering for all.

Imagining a Different Future

As government bureaucracy becomes more congealed and corporate banking more manipulative, money itself becomes more abstract and more illusive for human beings. Consequently, returning money-power to people will remain a central feature of the evolutionary lure being explored in Part Three of this book. As yet, it is unclear what shape this process will take. Perhaps, once again, a shift in consciousness has to happen first.

One attempt at a bold re-visioning of money for the future is that of the American philosopher, Charles Eisenstein (2011), who claims that nothing short of re-appropriating money as gift will fulfil the evolutionary aspirations of our time and rectify the financial mess we find ourselves in today. We are poised at a critical moment of opportunity to reclaim a gift culture, and therefore to build true community. The reclamation is part of a larger shift of human consciousness, an enhanced reunion with nature, earth, each other, and lost parts of ourselves. In a gift culture, people pass on their surplus rather than accumulate excess goods. Wealth circulates, gravitating toward the greatest need. In a gift community, people know that their gifts will eventually come back to them, frequently in a new form. Beyond the win-lose typical of the competitive monetized culture we know. People will be empowered into a win-win dynamic, where everybody benefits and so does the good fortune of the earth itself. We see evidence of this at work in Cuba's financial crisis of the early 1990s. (Webpage: http://en.wikipedia.org/wiki/Special_Period)

Towards an Alternative Economics

There are hundreds of online webpages describing a range of experiments that have been tried on how an alterative, more sustainable economic system would work. There is no shortage of creative ideas to inspire and encourage us to think differently. Authors such as Michael Albert, activist and political theorist, and Robin Hahnel, a radical economist, are names frequently associated with the notion of *participatory economics*. Seeking to involve both workers and consumers in all economic decisions, it prioritizes values such as equity, solidarity and mutual empowerment. It proposes four strategies for the implementation of its vision:

- *Workers and consumer councils* utilizing self-managerial methods for making decisions,
- *balanced job complexes*,
- *remuneration* according to effort and sacrifice, and
- *participatory planning*.

These principles operate in a number of well-known alternative experiments that have been extensively documented. These include The Mondragon Cooperative in Spain, Port Alegre in Brazil, The Grameen Bank in Bangladesh. Authors with a special interest in alternative economic systems, and keen to honor the evolutionary lure of the future, such as Bernard Lieter, Thomas Greco, and Charles Eisenstein, all cite several world-wide examples of creative alternatives, with the various fortunes that have befallen them. We certainly are not short of alternative, creative models. Why, then, have they not gained wider international recognition?

Albert and Hahnel acknowledge that novel economic strategies are unlikely to materialize without an accompanying reform of our dominant political and social institutions. There has to be an entire paradigm shift, involving not just some but all of the cultural entities that impact upon our daily living. This "all or nothing" emphasis is a factor in the notion of paradigm shifts that is unpalatable for the rational thinking still so pervasive in our modern world.

So, once again, we return to what now must surely be an enduring sense of hope for humanity and the earth itself: the evolutionary process will not be arrested, and the creative lure of the future will carry on, irrespective of whether humans come on board or not. We face a crucial and critical choice. We will need more than rational reason or academic know-how to embrace it. We'll need a whole new spirituality, the subject to which we next turn our attention.

28. *Spirituality: Reconnecting with the Empowering Spirit*

Be alert to the Lure: of the Great Spirit, weaving a trans-religious awakening, a synthesis of a very ancient wisdom, and a thrust of new hope for creation at large.

Spirituality affirms the ineffable divine as both the guiding intelligence and enlivening energy of the cosmos, to be found in the sacred sites of nature and of the self.

Gordon Lynch

Without an empowering spirituality, we will struggle to honor the lure of the future. Our anthropocentric self-reliance will not be adequate, nor is our inherited wisdom from formal religion likely to be of much use. In evolutionary terms, they both leave us with reductionistic answers, inadequate responses to the new questions of our time. Instead of being redeemed out of the world (religion's panacea) or wrestling with the future by more intense human control (the anthropocentric solution), we need a transpersonal vision grounding us in our earthly home while empowering us to rediscover it's inherent sacredness. We need a spirituality of engagement and not a devotion of escape.

While petrified masses rely afresh on a transcendent force to rescue us from the crisis of our time (the fundamentalist response), the more empowering spirituality is that which seeks meaning within the crisis and not outside it. Neither humans nor patriarchal Gods can rescue us from this evolutionary time characterized by both breakdown and breakthrough. We need a spirituality that can hold both in a creative paradoxical tension. *Rescuing* is a hopeless strategy that will only beget further despair. *Befriending* is the more authentic spiritual response and its challenge is what I want to explore in the present section

Several years ago, the Canadian theologian, Sallie McFague (1987; 1993), explored a restructuring of the Christian notion of the Trinity, suggesting that we re-vision the Creator as a Birthing Mother, Jesus as Lover, and the Holy Spirit as the Cosmic Befriender. Empowered by the Spirit of God who inhabits the whole of creation, we are invited and challenged to become involved in the Spirit's movement to renew all things in creation. The Spirit is God's outreach in befriending us through life's journey, and reciprocally, we are invited to enter into a loving relationship with everything the Spirit desires to make the world more lovable for all beings. This form of engagement is very real, a non-invasive and certainly a non-violent one.

From Religion to Spirituality

In Part Two of this book I outline some of the major differences between religion and spirituality –as each is understood today. Spirituality is rapidly outgrowing religion. Ideological forms of religion –the fundamental strands discernible in a number of the major religions, including Christianity and Islam –attracts a great deal of media attention, giving the impression that it is regaining cultural superiority. Fundamentalist religion has certainly gained fresh ground, mainly on the gullibility of fearful people. Once people become more educated –or simply aware of the forces generating their ideological fears –religion holds less meaning and significance for them.

As we move further into the twenty-first century, the lure of the future is likely to embrace spirituality rather than a revamped formal religion. As in many evolutionary shifts we are likely to witness new elements and ancient connections. What will be particularly baffling for religionists is the emergence of these new trends. They will not evolve logically from formal religions; evolution does not work in that way. Instead we will evidence quantum leaps that defy our logical, rational expectations. The new will feel like a reckless abandonment of that which has stood the test of time, and retrieval of ancient wisdom will be frequently condemned as a regression to infantile delusion.

To make sense of this new emergence it will be helpful to be deeply rooted and not merely clinging on to the established traditions of recent millennia. Acquaintance with the spiritual wisdom of indigenous peoples will be a useful starting-point, as will be more scholarly investigations into the deeper layers of wisdom –the archetypal truths – underpinning the great religions. Familiarity with a range of mystical traditions will prove to be a rich reservoir of spiritual enlightenment, provided we can access the mystical wisdom in its planetary and cosmic context –as attempted by Stace (1960) and Fox (1982), and not merely as another dimension of formal religion.

Since the 1960s, religious and social commentators have been observing the emergence of *a new mysticism*; one they suspect is linked with older expressions yet evolving through a range of new articulations. Many have noted a strong spiritual awakening coming through cosmology and science; others detect the lure through social and ecological activism, seeking justice not merely for humans but for the suffering earth itself. Sr. Joan Chittister has identified this awakening sense of the spiritual, in and through the material creation. In the opening words of her book on the New Spirituality she writes:

> There is a new question in the spiritual life; it is the spirituality of the spiritual life itself. Life here and how we relate to it, rather than life to come and how we guarantee it for ourselves, has become the spiritual conundrum of our age. (Chittister 1998, 1).

The focus has shifted from salvation for the immortal soul (divine rescue) in a world beyond, to liberation for all life forms through more empowering mutuality within the entire web of life. In several contexts, formal religions have tried to adopt this more expansive, engaging view, while still clinging to dualistic categories, ideologies of power, and outdated ideas like original sin and the end of the world. Those lured by the new spirituality detect too much old baggage in the attempts at religious revival; they seek new wineskins rather than trying to patch up the old system.

Coming Home to The Great Spirit

This yearning for something new and fresh tends to be denounced as reckless and irresponsible. I suspect it is an archetypal awakening that requires a great deal of discernment, and is more likely to make sense as a foundational allurement of our time. Sandra Schneiders in an oft-quoted article (Schneiders 1998) describes spirituality as the vital, ongoing interaction between the human spirit and the spirit of God, *with both poles receiving equal attention.* Spirituality is thus understood as spirit connecting with Spirit in something akin to a mutually enriching process. This explanation is significantly at variance with the irreconcilable differences typically portrayed in mainline religion. Schneiders hints at a common ground where both the human as well as divine spirit interface and interact in a spiritual symbiosis, thus suggesting a whole new foundation for spirituality at this time.

But is it totally new? Is she not describing a phenomenon highlighted in every indigenous faith-system known in our day: belief in the Great Spirit? And is this not a belief of great age itself, perhaps one of the most ancient forms of faith known to the human species?

In another book (O'Murchu 2012), I explore the significance of the Great Spirit. Here I merely cite some key elements. The Great Spirit denotes a divine life force that permeates and enlivens every fiber of creation, and while not restricted to the cosmic creation, is experienced within the energy flow of the entire universe. In mystical terms, it is awesome yet deeply intimate. It is not a personal God, yet embraces everything that is genuinely human and seeks the full flowering of everything in creation including the human.

Belief in the Great Spirit is devoid of any notion of worshipping a divine presence above and beyond this world. Instead it is requiring an enlightened alignment and intense engagement with the Spirit's creative energy impregnating and sustaining everything in creation. In Schneiders words, spirit seeks out Spirit, mutually engages with it, and collaboratively befriends evolution's lure for complexity and deeper growth.

The Spirituality of Pluralism

In the Asian context, spirituality today encounters a distinctive culture of pluralism. The interface with other major religions is inescapable, despite the fact that more fundamentalist Christian churches continue to denounce and ignore the emerging dialogue. And within the Great Eastern religions themselves –Buddhism, Hinduism, Islam –we observe a huge diversity including some disturbing reactionary developments in recent times.

The potential richness in multi-faith dialogue is still a largely unexplored territory. In fact more creative interaction has happened in the West rather than in the East, e.g., Christian-Buddhist dialogue. Modern Buddhism and Islam throughout the West have each morphed into a range of different expressions due to the interface with the West; some have been culturally enriching, others negative and reactionary. Throughout much of Asia, even where religions hold each other in love and admiration, relatively little inter-faith dialogue has taken place. Mobilizing inter-religious wisdom to advance justice and cultural enrichment, to embrace diversity, and advance healing and reconciliation, are still largely ideas that have been named, but little has been done to further their potential richness.

Beyond the rich and complex landscape of Asian religion, is the even more elaborate labyrinth of Asian spirituality. Once again, it has taken the expansion into the West to highlight the value and significance of Eastern meditation forms, such as yoga, Chinese and Japanese martial arts, ashrams, and a range of more esoteric practices involving spiritual gurus, lamas, mystics, spirit-guides and others. While we in the West associate earth-centered spirituality with tribal groups in the United States, Canada, Australia and Africa, such examples are at least equally as extensive throughout Asia, with several documented studies from the various regions of Polynesia.

The fear of homogenization

The contemporary study of spirituality seems to have an innate lure towards diversity and the celebration of commonalities. Instead of seeking differences that demarcate and separate, spirituality today initially seeks what cultures and peoples hold in common: moving further towards a search for a primordial covert unity underpinning the overt adversarial differences.

From formal religions, particularly Catholicism, this trend evokes the accusation of relativism. It perceives a risk of making relative those truths it claims to be exclusive and unique to one or other faith system. For example, Catholicism, and other fundamental Christian groups, claim that the uniqueness of Jesus is superior to all other divine "revelations" and therefore any attempt at seeking comparisons is automatically denounced as a form of relativism and a watering down of the uniqueness of the Christian position. I wish to alert the reader here to an important distinction between *uniqueness* and *superiority*. Certainly, contemporary spirituality readily acknowledges that Jesus is unique to Christianity just as Buddha is to Buddhism, or Mohamed to Islam, but to claim that one or other is superior to the rest is quite alien to modern spirituality. Indeed, it is viewed as a new and dangerous form of religious imperialism.

Additionally, is it a fear of homogenization? In our globalized world, everything tends to be flattened out towards a dull sameness. Fashions tend to be the same all over the globe, what some people call the "MacDonaldization" of culture. Emphasizing religious similarities, universalizing practices like Eastern-based meditation forms, or yoga practices, seeking to break down all religious divisions, feels like another attempt at making marketable religion/spirituality as a widely available commodity – sometimes sold for big money, as unfortunately has happened with the importation of some Eastern religious practices into the West.

The fear of homogenization is real, but often arises from ideological defensiveness than from genuine concern. In a world, so divided and polarized, any attempt at inviting people to explore commonalities and make difference mutually enriching (rather than polarizing) must surely be a welcome signal imbued with transcendent meaning. Even in conventional Christianity, the Holy Spirit is often viewed as a force for reconciliation, harmony and unity. If that Spirit is at the heart of the evolutionary lure of our time –as suggested above –then the call to this new synthesis requires of all a concerted effort at deeper discernment. On the quality of our response may depend not merely a more empowering spirituality for the future, but the more urgent choice for a viable human future on the earth itself.

From Religious Imperialism to Spiritual Befriending

The more religion clings on to dogmatic certainty and religious officialdom, the more it's going to lose its significance as a cultural value. In this time of global evolutionary change, many people feel fearful and apprehensive of the future. They want stronger religion, and clarity of teaching and doctrine. They seem to be holding the high moral ground, and driving a kind of fundamentalist revival. Defensive reactions of this type characterize all great evolutionary shifts. We feel safer with what we know, with what we presume has stood the test of time. The new feels scary and undermines our need for clarity and certainty.

Evolution is more likely to favor those who will venture out into broader horizons and embrace more risky endeavors. The lure of the future is already strongly endorsing the unfolding spirituality rather than formal religion. The Spirit who blows where she wills is certainly shaking up our staid foundations, and paradoxically not indicating one clear-cut alternative. It is a time to befriend the breakdown of the old, and the ensuing chaos. And befriending is also the strategy most conducive to our own survival – and thriving – in this turbulent but exciting time in which we are living.

Spiritual accompaniment is a skillful endeavor for this time. It requires not merely a training in the Ignatian method, but rather in a multi-disciplinary awareness through which we can hear the silent echoes deep within the evolutionary awakening itself, and explore ways to respond amid the chaos and confusion of our changing times. Such accompaniment will also be mutual, with several sources of wisdom being woven into our searching or exploring, and our daily conversations. We are all learners in this fragile, but empowering process, and the pioneering wisdom of the Spirit is likely to be more engaging where the two or three gather at Wisdom's footstool.

≈ ◇ ≈

29. *Catholicism and the Lure of the Future*

Be alert to the Lure of a new global Church, with people to the fore.

I continue to hope that Catholic educators will resist a lapse into religious fundamentalism and become instead a shining example of the virtues so necessary for our common future –a love for the world as we empirically find it, and a sense that everything in it is holy.

Chet Raymo

Since many of the readers of this book are likely to have links with the Catholic Church, I offer this final section on the evolutionary challenges facing modern Catholicism. My hope is that these reflections will also be useful for people of other Christian persuasions.

In popular media, the Catholic Church tends to be portrayed as conservative, legalistic, preoccupied with its own power structure, and dismissive of all who disagree with its moral and doctrinal teachings. The Catholic "position"is nearly always portrayed as the official teaching from the Pope, transmitted down through the clerical hierarchical structure of the Church. All too often the reader is left with the impression that the Catholic people are passively submissive, with a military sense of obedience to those at the top.

Not merely is this an unfair depiction, it is also grossly inaccurate. Ironically, there are millions of Catholics who never challenge the stereotype, either through fear, reticence, or the risk of being interpreted as being anti-Church. The true picture is much more complex, and to the vast surprise of many people - including Catholics –the Catholic faith community has been lured into an evolutionary emergence that could radically change Catholicism in just a matter of decades.

The Catholic paradigm shift

I want to highlight three features of modern Catholicism that indicate an irretrievable shift with significant implications for both the short and long term future.

> *1. Demographic Shift*: In 1960, 66% of Catholics lived in the white Western World, with only 34% in the South. Today 80% live in the South and only 20% in the North. Various sociological explanations can be offered, but my interest is primarily theological, provoking the question: *is the Holy Spirit pioneering this movement?* Once we answer positively, which I do, then Catholicism today faces a challenge of discernment, unprecedented in the history of the past 2,000 years.

> The Holy Spirit is luring the Catholic Church into the twenty-first century, co-creating a Church that is predominantly non-Caucasian, multi-cultural, poor and struggling for justice. There are new heart centers coming into being in this new Catholic family: *Nigeria, Brazil and the Philippines*. Focusing on *Rome* makes no sense anymore – Rome is at the heart of the dying Church of Europe. And to illustrate, the inflexibility of the Catholic leadership, two-thirds of the Bishops still dwell in the North, while 80% of people live in the South.

> *2. The People-Priest ratio*: Critics often condemn the Catholic Church as a priest-ridden institution. In fact, the total number of ordained priests is less than 500,000 out of a Catholic population of 1.2 billion people. That translates into 99.95% lay people with priests comprising a mere 00.05%. There certainly is a clerical sub-culture that still bedevils Catholicism, but much more significantly, is the growing body of people, who think for themselves, reflect critically,

read and dialogue, and no longer behave in the co-dependent fashion of just a few years ago.

In terms of formal Church membership, there is a disturbing trend. Many of the most reflective Catholics tend to move out of formal membership, or adopt a lose sense of affiliation from the periphery. However, as noted elsewhere in this book, it is the shifting consciousness that is likely to foretell a different and possibly more engaging future. Catholic consciousness is increasingly that of reflective, critical engagement, with many more people adopting an adult stance and demanding a form of engagement conducive to adult growth and development.

3. A New Theological Threshold. The Council of Trent in the sixteenth century reserved the study of theology only to priests and clerical students, and that regulation remained strictly in place till about 1960. Of all Catholics studying theology in 1970, an estimated 5% were lay people. Today at least 60% of Catholic theologians are lay, and that percentage continues to rise. Not merely is the priest theologian a dwindling species, but more significantly, lay people themselves invest more trust in the wisdom of the lay theologian than in that of the priest.

Even the enlightened priest theologian is still primarily concerned about the internal matters of Church life, relating to sacraments, church order, and morality. The lay theologian tends to be focused on the major questions facing humanity on a global scale, leading to the interface of theology and economics, theology and politics, theology and environment, theology and globalization. For the lay theologian, theology is going global while also being one of the most inter-disciplinary fields of research both now and for the future.

The View from the Future

All the Christian Churches claim to be founded in the power of the Holy Spirit as the chief mediator of wisdom from on high. It looks like it might be the Great Spirit who is shaking the tired foundations of the Catholic Church and inaugurating a novel Catholic identity, which is as global and complex as the Spirit who blows where it wills. While Catholic leadership expends a great deal of time and energy regressing to the Roman inheritance (Latin language, etc.) the people's Church is diversifying into a new cultural entity in the Southern hemisphere, immersed in the hopes and dreams of a largely youthful population.

Thus far, the enculturation in the South is largely mimicking the Roman imperialism of the North, and in several cases, clerics impose a heavy hand, rarely witnessed in other places. However, if the Holy Spirit is behind and within this new movement – and I certainly believe she is – then all the human resistance on earth will not hinder the Pentecostal fire that the Spirit will ignite.

This is how the evolutionary lure works, defying all our rational expectations and undermining even the most robust resistance. This is not some wild utopian dream — but an outrageous sense of hope, which is what the evolutionary lure awakens time and again. Assuredly the awakening will be chaotic and confusing, like birth pangs. But it will transpire, and for Catholic people of the future it holds a dream full of promise, not merely for Catholicism itself, but for every cultural engagement ensuing from it.

≈ ◇ ≈

Fourth Benchmark: *Learning to flow with Evolution's Rhythm*

Humanity's greatest hope rests in the thrust of evolution itself. Come what may; emergence and becoming will continue unabated. We cannot stop the process of evolution nor can we alter its increasing acceleration and intensified complexity. The momentum for growth and expansion will gain greater speed, and enrich our existence with a deepening sense of complexity.

As to where it will eventually lead us is a wisdom beyond our current comprehension, a plight that the learned and powerful of our world will never accept. A virulent anthropocentricism still holds its grip on a sector of the human family who feel that they possess some kind of a God-given right to rule the universe. For them, all this talk about evolution is a kind of esoteric speculation, which they ridicule and seek to undermine. It poses a threat to their power, and therefore it must be discredited.

Scientists occupy a particularly ambivalent space. They acknowledge and affirm the evolutionary nature of life on both the macro and micro levels of existence. Yet they consign humans to a kind of suspended superiority above and beyond the life-processes they explore so thoroughly. Even those who acknowledge that humanity today is on a dangerously slippery slope, still cling on to the notion of an anthropocentric privilege that exalts and inflates our status as evolutionary creatures.

Evolution will continue –with or without us. We have a basic choice, which some will view with cold fatalism and others comprehend as endowed with mystical potential. We can resist the flow of evolutionary becoming, and in that case we become its helpless victims, condemning ourselves to anomie and despair. Or we can choose to flow with its rhythms and creative possibilities for a different future, and therefore we will stand some chance of becoming its beneficiaries. This in itself does not guarantee a viable future, but at the very least it assures us some semblance of being able to die with dignity. That is an evolutionary choice, which may have more life-promising potential than has been generally recognized to date.

The reflections of this book seek to honor our past, present, and future. We are creatures on a continuum, and movement is our default position, the paradox of the wave-particle duality articulated in quantum physics. From the *past*, we have much to learn. In the *present* time, we strive to remain connected and engaged, rather than hiding in the shadows of denial. And faithful to the empowering vision of the great mystics (in all religions) we open ourselves to the lure of the *future*.

This enlarged context, with the accompanying invitation to become participants and not mere spectators, illuminates many of the deeper truths that have sustained humanity through several past transitions. These are the truths that our patriarchal cultures have consigned to mainline religion. That historical container is no longer adequate; the inculturated truths have broken lose into the wider environment of our cultural and spiritual experience. Truth endures but in the morphed spiritual expressions congenial to the evolutionary awakening that is transpiring all over planet Earth today.

Without this empowering spirituality, the journey will not be easy. The same Spirit who evoked meaning and beauty from the original chaos of creation is once more reweaving the patterns within the evolving web of life. Our spiritual attunement to that Spirit is probably our single greatest resource for the transitions we experience, and our surest guide to the future opening up before us. Under the enduring wisdom of that Great Spirit, we venture forth.

≈ ◇ ≈

Bibliography

Adams, Daniel J. (1997), "Toward a Theological Understanding of Postmodernism," *Cross Currents,* Vol. 47, 518-530.

Anderson, Chris. 2006. *The Long Tail: Why the Future of Business Is Selling Less of More.* New York: Hyperion.

Bauman, Z. 2003. *Liquid Love: on the Frailty of Human Bonds,* Cambridge (UK): Polity Press.

Berry, Thomas 1985. "Bioregions: The Context for Reinhabiting the Earth," *Breakthrough*, Spring/Summer, 6-9.

Brock, Rita N. and Rebecca Parker. 2008. *Saving Paradise.* Boston: Beacon Press.

Brueggemann, Walter. 1986. *Hopeful Imagination*, Philadelphia: Fortress Press.

Cannato, Judy. 2006. *Radical Amazement,* Notre Dame, Ind.: Sorin Books.

Chalmers, David. 1996. *The Conscious Mind: In Search of a Fundamental Theory.* New York: Oxford University Press.

Chittister, Joan. 1998. *Heart of Flesh*, Mi.: Grand Rapids.

Church, Dawson. 2007. *The Genie in Your Genes.* Fulton, Ca.: Psychology Books.

De Bono, Edward.1970. *Lateral thinking: Creativity Step by Step.* New York: Harper & Row.

_____. 1992. *Serious Creativity: Using the Power of Lateral Thinking to Create New Ideas.* New York: Harper & Row.

Dennett, Daniel.1993. Consciousness Explained. New York: Penguin.

De Waal, Frans .2010. *The Age if Empathy: Nature's Lessons for a Kinder Society,*

Douthwaite, Richard.1998. *Short Circuit: Practical New Approach in Building more Self-reliant Communities.* London: Green Books.

Ekins, Paul and Manfred Max-Neef. EDS. 1992. *Real-Life Economics: Understanding Wealth Creation.* New York: Routledge.

Eisenstein, Charles. 2011. *Sacred Economics*, Berkeley, CA: Evolver Editions.

Falk, Richard. 2001. *Religion and Humane Global Governance.* New York: Pelgrave.

Fox, Matthew. 1982. *Original Blessing: A Primer in Creation Spirituality*, Santa Fe: bear & Co.

Giddens, Anthony. 1991. *Modernity and Self-image,* Cambridge (UK): Polity Press.

Greco, Thomas. 2009. *The End of Money*, Edinburgh: Floris Books.

Harris, Sam. 2005. *The End of Faith: religion, Terror and the Future of Reason*, London: Free Press.

Hart, Donna, and Robert W. Sussman. 2005. *Man the Hunted: Primates, Predators and Human Evolution.* New York: Basic Books.

Haught, John F. 2000. *God After Darwin,* Westminster John Knox Press.

_____. 2010. *Making Sense of Evolution: Darwin, God and the Drama of Life*, Westminster John Knox Press.

Hawken, Paul. 2007. *Blessed Unrest.* New York: Penguin/ Viking.

Hill, Jason. 2002. *On Being a Cosmoplitan.* Lanham, Md.: Rowman & Littlefield.

Hines, Colin. 2000. *Localization: A Global Manifesto.* London: Earthscan Publications.

Hrdy, Sarah Blaffer. 2009. *Mothers and Others: The Evolutionary Origins of Mutual Understanding.* Cambridge, Mass: Harvard University Press.

Jantsch, Erich. 1980. *The Self-organizing Universe*, New York: Pergamon Press.

Kaufmann, Stuart A. 1993. *The Origins of Order.* New York: Oxford University Press

Keltner, Dacher & Alia. 2010. *The Compassionate Instinct*, New York: W.W. Norton.

Korten, David C. 2006. *The Great Turning: From Empire to Earth Community*, San Francisco: Berrett-Koehler.

Kurzweil, Ray. 2005. *The Singularity is Near*, New York: Viking.

Leakey, Richard and Roger Lewin. 1996. *The Sixth Extinction: Biodiveristy and its Survival.* London: Weidenfeld & Nicolson.

Lewis-Williams, David. 2002. *The Mind in the Cave*, London: Thames & Hudson.

Lietaer, Bernard. 2002. *The Future of Money*, London: Century Books.

Lifton, Robert J. 1999. *The Protean Self.* Chicago: University of Chicago Press.

Lipton, Bruce 2005. *The Biology of Belief.* Santa Rosa, Ca.: Elite Books.

Lovelock, James. 1979. *Gaia: A New Look at Life on Earth.* Oxford (UK): Oxford University Press.

_____. 1988. *The Ages of Gaia*, Oxford (UK): Oxford University Press.

Madigan, Kevin and Jon D. Levenson. 2008. *Resurrection: The Power of God for Christians and Jews*, New Haven, Ct.: Yale University Press.

Margulis, Lynn. 1998. *The Symbiotic Planet.* New York: basic Books.

McFague, Sallie. 1987. *Models of God*, Philadelphia: Fortress Press.

_____. 1993. *The Body of God: An Ecological Theology*, London: SCM Press.

McTaggart, Lynn. 2007. *The Intention Experiment,* New York: Free Press.

Meadows, Donella & Alia. 1972. *The Limits of Growth.* New York: Signet.

_____. 2004. *The Limits of Growth: The 30-Year Update*, White River Junction, VT: Chelsea Green.

Meyer, M.W. and L.G. Zucker. 1989. *Permanently Failing Organizations*. London: Sage Publications.

Midgley, Mary. 2010. *The Solitary Self: Darwin and the Selfish Gene*. Durham (UK): Acumen Publishing.

O'Murchu, Diarmuid. 2004. *Quantum Theology*, New York: Crossroad.

_____. 2009. *Ancestral Grace*, Maryknoll, N Y: Orbis Books

_____. 2010. *Adult Faith*, Manila: Claretian Publications.

_____. 2011. *Christianity's Dangerous Memory*, Manila: Claretian Publications

_____.2012. *In the Beginning was the Spirit*. Maryknoll, NY: Orbis Books.

Pearce, Jospeh Chilton. 2002. *The Biology of Transcendence*. South Paris, Me.: Park Street Press.

Raymo, Chet. 2008. *When God is Gone, Everything is Holy*. Notre Dame, In.: Ave Maria Press.

Rifkin, Jeremy. 2009. *The Empathic Civilization*, Cambridge (UK): Polity.

Ross, M.M. (2000), "Towards a Renewal of Theology in India through Postmodernism,"*Indian Journal of Theology*, 42, 192-203.

Roszak, Theodore. 2009. *The Making of an Elder Culture*. Gabriola Island, Bc.: New Society Publishers.

Roughgarden, Joan. 2009. *The Genial Gene*. San Francisco: University of California Press.

Russell, Peter. 1982. *The Awakening Earth,* London: Arkana.

Sale, Kirkpatrick. 1991. *Dwellers in the Land*. San Francisco: Sierra Club.

Schneiders, Sandra.1998. 'The Study of Christian Spirituality: Contours and Dynamics of a Discipline,' *Christian Spirituality Bulletin,* Vol. 6, No. 1 (Spring 1998).

Schroeder, Gerald. 2001. *The Hidden face of God: How Science Reveals the Ultimate Truth,* New York: Free Press.

Sheldrake, Rupert. 2009. *Morphic Resonance: The Nature of Formative Causation*, South Paris, ME: Park Street Press.

Sorokin, Pitirim 1957. *Social and Cultural Dynamics: A Study of Change in Major Systems of Art, Truth, Ethics, Law and Social Relationships.* Boston: Extending Horizons Books.

Spretnak, Charlene. 1992. *States of Grace.* San Francisco: Harper.

Stace, Walter. 1960. *The Teaching of the Mystics.* New York: New American Library.

Swimme, Brain and Thomas Berry. 1992. *The Universe Story.* San Francisco: Harper.

Suzuki, David. 2002. *The Sacred Balance: Rediscovering our Place in Nature.* Vancouver: Douglas & McIntyre.

Tarlow, Mikela and Philip. 2002. *Digital Aboriginal: The Direction of Business Now.* New York: Time Warner Books.

Taylor, Steve. 2005. The Fall. Ropley (UK): O Books.

van Lommel, Pim. 2010, *Consciousness Beyond Life.* New York: Harper One.

Welwood, John (2007), *Perfect Love, Imperfect Relationships,* Boston, Ma.: Shambala Publications.

Wheatley, Margaret J. 1992. *Leadership and the New Science.* San Francisco: Berrett-Koehler.

Wilshire, Bruce. 1998. *Wild Hunger.* Oxford (UK): Rowman & Littlefield.

Wilson Schaef, Anne. 1988. *When Society Becomes an Addict,* New York: HarperOne.